기본기를 다지기 위한

Practical English

김 태 훈

YOUNG MIN PUBLISH
도서출판 영민

토익과 친해지기

Reading Comprehension

1. 단문 공란 메우기

빈칸이 들어간 하나의 문장을 보고 4개의 선택지 중에서 빈칸에 알맞은 것을 고르는 문제.

풀이전략 - 품사나 문장의 구조와 같이 영어의 기본개념을 완벽히 이해한 후, 부정사, 동명사 등 특정 형태의 문법 규칙을 학습, 암기하도록 한다. 또한 다양한 어휘의 뜻을 얼마나 정확하게 알고 있는지를 묻는 문제로, 개별 어휘의 기본 의미뿐만이 아니라 어휘가 갖고 있는 뉘앙스나 어법을 묻는 고난도 문제들도 출제된다.

2. 독해

주어진 한 개 혹은 두 개의 지문을 읽고 제시된 2-5개의 질문에 알맞은 답을 고르는 문제.

풀이전략 – 대부분의 지문은 비즈니스 상황이나 일상생활에서 접할 수 있는 문서들이다. 평소에 이런 상황에서 주고 받을 수 있는 문서의 유형과 형식에 익숙해지는 것이 가장 중요하다. 특정 단어나 어구를 변환하여 이해를 흐리는 경우는 다양한 어휘를 숙지하여 해결하도록 한다.

목차

제1강

단어와 품사

단어 — 한 언어에 있어 의미를 가진 가장 작은 단위

품사 — 마트에 가면 상품을 코너 별로 구분해서 전시한 것처럼 단어를 쓰임에 따라 분류한 것

각 품사별 정의 및 문장에서 쓰이는 성분

순서	품사	하는 역할	문장성분
1	명사	모든 것을 부르는 말	주어 / 목적어 / 보어
2	대명사	명사 대신 쓰는 말	주어 / 목적어 / 보어
3	동사	움직임, 상태를 나타내는 말	동사
4	형용사	명사를 꾸며주거나, 설명해주는 역할 (쓰레기, 필수성분 보어)	보어
5	부사	adverb 주로 동사를 꾸며준다 (쓰레기)	성분이 될 수 없다.
6	전치사	명사와 한 덩어리 = 전명구는 형용사, 부사의 역할을 한다 (쓰레기)	성분이 될 수 없다.
7	접속사	연결하는 역할	성분이 될 수 없다.

품사를 구별해서 풀 수 있는 문제가 문법 문제의 35%를 차지합니다. (토익 최신 경향 기준) 점수 배점으로 약 60점에 해당하는 부분이니 꼭 단어를 품사별로 구분하는 연습을 해야 합니다.

특히, 한 어휘에 여러 품사가 있는 것에 주의하세요.

줄임말 안내

명사	noun	n.
동사	verb	v.
형용사	adjective	a.
부사	adverb	ad.

품사 구분하기

시험에 출제되는 모든 단어를 외우면 좋습니다.

그렇지 못한 경우에 대비하여 **명사, 동사, 형용사, 부사**를 알려주는 형태를 알아봅시다.

제2강

단어의 형태와 품사 구분하기

▎명사를 알려주는 꼬리

꼬리		예
− tion		resignation regulation
− sure		closure pleasure
− ty		specialty necessity
− ance		acceptance
− ness		kindness happiness
사람	− ant − ent	applicant assistant attendant ex) flight attendant
	− ist − yst	analyst pianist
	− er − or	advisor manager
− al		denial renewal

▎동사를 알려주는 꼬리

꼬리	예
− ze	familiarize minimize
− fy	specify notify satisfiy
− en	streghten widen lengthen

▎형용사를 알려주는 꼬리

꼬리	예
− ful	thoughtful successful
− ble	able possible
− al	national operational
− ic	specific
− ous	dangerous famous
명사 + ly	yearly quarterly monthly weekly daily
− ive	expensive
− ry	advisory satisfactory
− ent	evident

▎부사를 알려주는 꼬리

꼬리	예
형용사 +ly	specifically publicly

품사 구별 필살기 자료 — 외우지 말고, 자주 읽어보는 습관을 가집시다.

authorization n. 승인
authorize v. 승인해주다

display n. 전시품; v. 전시하다
displayable a. 전시할 수 있는
on display 전시 중

happy a. 행복한
happily ad. 행복하게
happiness n.행복

strict a. 엄격한
strictly ad. 엄격히
strictness n. 엄격함

remark v. ~에 주목하다; 말하다
remarkably ad.현저하게, 눈에 띄게

perfect a. 완벽한; 완성하다
perfectly ad. 완벽하게
perfection n. 완벽함

emphatic a. 어조가 강한
emphasis n. 강조

★
length n. 길이
lengthy a. 긴, 장황한
lengthily ad. 길게
lengthen v. 길게 하다

assist v. 돕다
assistant n.조수, 보좌인
assistance n.도움, 보조

dedication n. 헌신, 전념
dedicated a. 전념하는
delicately ad. 우아하게, 섬세하게

purposeless a. 무의미한
purposeful a. 목적이 있는
purposely ad. 고의로, 일부러

access n. 접근 v. 접근하다
accessible a. 접근할 수 있는
accessibility n. 접근성

specify v. 일일이 열거하다,
specification n. 상술, 열거
specifically ad. 특히, 특별히
specific a. 상세한

single a. 단 하나의
singly ad. 단독으로

modify v. 개조하다
modification n. 개조

locate v. ~장소를 알아내다, 찾아내다
be located at/ in/ on v.~에 ~위치하다
locations n. 위치, 장소

promise v. 약속하다 n. 약속
promising a. 유망한

★
close v. 닫다 a. 가까운, 친밀한
closely ad. 가까이, 접근하여

distribute v. 분배하다
distributor n. 분배자, 배급[배포]자
distribution n. 분배, 배급, 배포

regard v. ~을 (…으로) 간주하다, 여기다
regarding 전치사. = about ~관하여

final n. 최후의 것
finally ad. 드디어
final a. 최후의, 마지막의
finalist n. 결승전 출장 선수
finalize v. 마무리 짓다

open v. 열다, a. 열려있는
opener n. 병따개, n. 여는 사람
opening n. 공석, 빈자리

exception n. 예외
exceptional a. 뛰어난, 예외적인
exceptionally ad. 예외적으로, 매우

urgent a. 긴급한
urgency n. 긴급 사항

train v. 교육하다
training n. 교육, 훈련

confirmation n. 확인(서)
confirm v. 확인하다

respect v. 존경심, 존경하다
respectable a. 존경할 만한

enthusiasm n. 열광, 열중
enthusiastic a. 열광적인, 열렬한
enthusiastically ad. 열광적으로
enthuse v. 열중하다
enthusiast n. 열광자, 광팬

attentive a. 귀를 귀울이는
attention n. 주의, 집중
attentively ad. 주의 깊게
attentiveness n. 주의력

expenses n. 돈, 비용
expensive a. 값 비싼
expensively ad. 비싸게
extract n. 발췌 v. 추출하다, 뽑다
extractable a. 추출할 수 있는

indicate v. 나타내다
indicative a. 암시하는
indication n. 암시

authenticate v. 진짜임을 증명하다
authentic a. 진짜의, 원본의
authenticity ad. 확실성, 신뢰성

★
specialize v. 전문화하다
specialized a. 전문의
specialization n. 특수화
cf) specialize in: ~에 전문이다

delighted: a. 기쁜 감정을 느끼는
delightful a. 기쁜, 신난
delightfully ad. 기쁘게
delight v. 기쁘게 하다

widely ad. 널리
widen v. 넓히다

invest v. 투자하다
investment n. 투자

history n. 역사
historian n. 역사가
historical a. 역사상의
historically ad. 역사적으로

innovate v. 혁신하다, 쇄신하다
innovative a. 혁신적인, 쇄신적인
innovation n. 혁신

founder n.창설자
found v. 설립하다
founded a. 기초한
profit n. 이익 (셀 수 있는 명사)
v.이익이 되다
profitable a. 이익이 되는
profitability n. 수익성

sincerely ad. 진정으로
sincerity n. 성실
sincere a. 진심의

energy n. 에너지
energize v.격려하다, 힘 나게 하다
energetic a. 활기 찬
energetically ad. 활기차게

acquaint v. 알리다, 숙지시키다
cf) be acquainted with: ~를 잘 알다
acquaintance n. 아는 사람

publicity n. 광고, 선전
publicize v. 광고하다, 선전하다
notice v. 알아차리다 n. 공지 사항
noticeable a. 현저한
noticeably ad. 현저하게

approve v. 승인하다
approval n. 승인, 인가
approvable a. 승인 할 수 있는

impress v. 감명을 주다
impressive a. 인상적인
impressed a. 감동받은 (사람수식)
be impressed with/ by ~에 감동한

necessity n. 필요성; 필수품
necessary a. 필요한
necessarily n. 반드시
necessitate v. 필요로 하다

subsequently ad. 이어서, 그 후에
subsequent a. 다음의, 그 후의
subsequent to 전. ~후에
subsequence n. 계속일어남 연속.

character n. 성격
characteristic n. (가산명사) 특성
characteristically ad. 특징적으로

vital a. 극히 중대한
vitally ad. 치명적으로
vitality n. 생명력
vitalize v. 생명을 주다

cooperate v. 협력하다
cooperative a. 협력의

quickly ad. 신속히
quick a. 신속한

recommend v.제안하다, 추천하다
recommendation n. 제안; 추천
highly recommended 강추 되는
confide v. 신임하다, 신뢰하다
confidential a. 기밀의

direction n. 방향, 지시사항
directly ad. 바로, 직접적으로
direct v. 지도하다

universal a. 보편적인
universe n. 우주
universally ad. 보편적으로
universality n. 일반성

invite v.초대하다
invitation n. 초대, 초대장

value v.가치 평가하다 n. 가치
valuable a. 소중한, 가치 있는
valuably ad. 소중하게

potent a. 강력한
potential n. 잠재력
potentially ad. 잠재적으로
potentiality n. 가능성
potential 을 주로 명사로 쓴다,

renovation n. 보수, 수리 혁신
renovate v. 보수하다

efficient a.효율적인
efficiency n. 효율성
efficiently ad. 효율적으로

care v. 돌봄 보살피다
careful a.조심성 있는
carefully ad. 신중히, 조심스럽게
cared a. 걱정되는

produce v. 생산하다
productively ad. 생산적으로
productivity n. 생산성

serve v. 봉사하다
servings n. 음식 시중, 접대

impress n. 인상을 주다
impressive a. 인상 깊은
impressively ad. 인상적으로

moderately ad. 적당히
moderate a. 적당한, 보통의, 알맞은
moderator n. 중재자, 조절자

diversity n. 다양성
diverse a. 다양한
diversify v. 다양화하다, 다각화하다

prompt a. 즉각적인
promptly ad. 즉시
promptness n. 즉시성

increase v. 증가하다 n. 증가
increasing a. 증가하는
increasingly ad. 더욱 더, 점점

prevent v. 막다
preventive a. 예방적인
prevented a. 방해된

receive v. 받다
receivable a. 받아야 할, 믿을만한
receipt n. 영수증
n. 받음
recipient n. 받는 사람

supply v. 공급하다;
n. 공급품, 준비품
supplier n. 공급업자, 공급업체

allow v. 허락하다
allowable a. 허락할 수 있는
allowance n. 수당 (허락 아님)

★
complete a. 완벽한
v. 완료하다
completely ad. 완벽히

schedule n. 예정, 계획;
v. 예정하다
scheduled a. 예정된

deliver v. 배송하다, 배달하다
delivery n. 배송, 배달
deliverable a. 배달 가능한
deliverer n. 배달자

plan v. 계획하다 n. 계획
planner n. 계획자
planning n. 계획
planned a. 계획된

advisable a. 권할 만한, 타당한
advisory a. 조언하는, 권고하는
advisedly ad. 신중하게
advise v. 조언하다, 충고하다

evenly ad. 고르게
even ad. ① (비교급 강조) 더 ~한
② 심지어

recommend v. 추천하다
recommendation n. 추천
responsible a. 책임이 있는
be responsible for ~에 책임 있는
responsibility n. 책무, 책임
responsibly ad. 책임감 있게

depend v. 의존하다
depend on ~에 의존하다
dependable a. 의지할 수 있는
dependence n. 의존
dependent a. 에 달려있는, 의존하는
dependability n. 의존할 수 있음

confirm v. 확인하다
confirmation n. 확인

promote v. 홍보하다, 승진시키다
promotion n. 촉진, 승진
promotional a. 홍보의, 승진의

complete v. 완성하다, 완료하다.
a. 완성된
completion n. 완성, 완료
completely ad. 완전히

ease n. 쉬움, 편함
easy a. 쉬운
easily ad. 쉽게

contract n. 계약 v. 계약하다
contractor n. 계약인, 계약받은 사람

sharp a. 날카로운
sharpen v. 날카롭게 하다
sharply ad. 급격하게, 날카롭게
sharpness n. 날카로움

★
economy n. 경제
economist n. 경제학자
economize v. 절약하다
경제적으로 사용하다
economical a. 경제적인, 절약하는
economic a. 경제의

identify v. 확인하다
identity n. 동일함, 일체성
identifiable a. (신원을) 확인할 수 있는
동일함을 증명할 수 있는

expect v. 기대하다
expectations n. 기대
expectant a. 기대하는

clear a. 명백한
clearly ad. 명료하게, 분명하게
clarity n. (문체, 사상의) 명쾌함, 명석함
clarify v. 명백히 하다

effect n. 결과, 효과 초래하다
effective a. 효과적인
effectively ad. 효과적으로
effectiveness n. 유효(성), 효과적임

inaccuracy n. 부정확, 틀림
inaccurate a. 부정확한
inaccurately ad. 잘못되게 부정확하게

increase v. 증가하다 n. 증가
increasingly ad. 점점, 더욱 더
increasing a. 증가하는

approve v. 승인하다, 찬성하다
approval n. 승인
approvingly ad. 찬성하여
prefer v. 선호하다
preference n. 선호하는 것, 선호물
preferred a. 선호되는, 우선의

limit v. 제한하다; n. 제한
limited a. 한정된, 제한된
limitation n. 제한

predict v. 예보하다
prediction n. 예언
predictable a. 예언할 수 있는
predictably ad. 예언할 수 있게, 당연하게

contribute v. 기여하다, 공헌하다
contribute to ~ing ~에 공헌하다
contribution n. 기여, 공헌
contributor n. 공헌자

complicate v. 복잡하게 하다
★ complicated a. 복잡한
complicatedly ad. 복잡하게

ready a. 준비된
readily ad. 손쉽게, 즉석에서
readiness n. 준비, 신속

qualify v. 자격을 부여하다
참고: qualify for ~자격을 갖추다
qualified a. 자격이 있는
qualifier n. 자격을 주는 사람
qualification n. 자격

provided a. 준비된, 제공된
provider n. 공급업체
provision n. 준비
provide v. 제공하다, 공급하다
참고: provide A with B A 에게 B 를 제공하다

consider v. 숙고하다
considerate a. 사려 깊은
★considerable a. 상당한; 중요한
★considerably ad. 상당히, 꽤

vacant a. 빈, 세든 사람이 없는
vacantly ad. 멍하니, 멀거니
vacancy n. 공백: 빈자리 : 빈 방
vacate v. (집·방·자리)를 비우다;~에서 떠나다

participate v. 참가하다
참고: participate in ~에 참석하다
participant n. 참가자

please v. 기쁘게 하다
pleased a. 만족 스러운, 기쁜
be pleased with ~로 기쁜
be pleased toV ~하게 되어 기쁜
pleasant a. 즐거운
pleasure n. 기쁨, 즐거움

detail n. 세부사항; v. 상술하다
detailed a. 자세한
in detail 자세히

brief a. 간략한, 짧은
briefly ad. 짧게

reside v. 거주하다, 살다
resident n. 거주자
a. 거주 하는, 살고 있는
residence n. 거주, 주택

continue v. 계속하다
continuity n. 연속, 계속
continuous a. 계속하는
continuously ad. 끊임없이, 계속적

★ complain v. 불평하다, 불만을 말하다
complain 은 명사 아님!! 동사!
complaints n. 항의, 불평, 불만
complainer n. 불평하는 사람

disappoint v. 실망시키다
disappointed a. 실망한
disappointment n. 실망
disappointing a. 실망스러운,

equal a. 동등한, 같은
equally ad. 동등하게
equality n. 동등함
equalize v. 동등하게 하다,

profit n. 이익
profitable a. 이익이되는, 유익한

adapt v. 적응시키다
adaptation n. 각색, 번안

frequent a. 빈번한
frequency n. 빈발; 빈도
frequently ad. 종종, 자주

exhibit v. 진열하다
exhibition n. 전시회
exhibitor n. 출품자

attract v. (주의, 관심을) 끌다, 유인하다
attraction n. 매력, 관광명소
참고: tourist attraction 관광명소
attractive a. 매력 있는

★ leading a. 선두의
leader n. 지도자
lead v. 이끌다
leadership n. 리더십

certification n. 증명; 증명서
certificate n. 증명서; 학위
certify v. 증명하다

hesitate v. 망설이다
hesitance n. 망설임, 주저
hesitant a. 주저하는
hesitantly ad. 주저하며

succession n. 계승
successive a. 연속 하는, 잇따르는
successor n. 계승자
succeed v. 계승하다, 성공하다
succeed v. 성공하다, 계속되다, 잇따르다.
successful a. 성공한
successfully ad. 성공적으로
success n. 성공

depend v. 의존하다
dependence n. 의지, 신뢰
dependent a. 의존하는
dependently ad. 의존하고 있는
decide v. 결정하다
decision n. 결정
decisive a. 결정적인, 중대한
decidedly ad. 확실히, 명백히

quiet a. 조용한
quietly ad. 조용히

benefit n. 이익, 이득;
v. 이익이 되다
beneficially ad. 유익하게
beneficial a. 이익이 되는

recently ad. 최근에
recent a. 최근의

prohibit v. 금하다, 금지하다
prohibition n. 금지

insist v. 주장하다
insisting a. 주장하는, 고집하는
insistent a. 강요하는, 고집하는

express v. 표현하다
expressive a. 표현하는
expressly ad. 명확히

investigate v. 조사하다
investigated a. 조사된
investigation n. 조사
investigator n. 조사자
investigative a. 조사의

suit v. 적합하게 하다
suitable a. 적절한
be suitable for ~에 적합한
suitably ad. 적절하게

strategize v. 전략을 세우다
strategy n. 전략
strategic a. 전략적인
strategically ad. 전략적으로

lose v. 잃다
loss n. 손실
lost a. 잃은 v. 잃었다
losing a. 손해 보는; 실패, 패배

attendance n. 참석, 참석율
attend v. 참석하다
attendee n. 참석자, (호텔, 주차장 등의) 안내원

expect v. 예상하다, 기대하다
expectation n. 예상, 기대

update v. 개정하다, 갱신하다
updated a. 최신의, 개정된

reputably ad. 평판 좋게
reputable a. 평판이 좋은
repute n. 평판; 명성
reputation n. 평판; 명선

★
implementation n. 이행, 수행
implement v. 이행하다, 수행하다

competitor n. 경쟁자, 경쟁 업체
competitive a. 경쟁의
competitiveness n. 경쟁력, 경쟁적임
competitively ad. 경쟁적으로

spend v. 소비하다
spender n. (돈을) 소비하는 사람
spending n. 소비, 지출

kind a. 친절한
kindly ad. 친절하게, 마음씨 고운

construct v. 건설하다
constructive a. 건설적인
construction n.건설, 공사

large a. 큰
largely ad. 크게, 대대적으로

appreciation n. 감사
appreciative a.감사의; 감상하는
appreciate v. 감사하다

probable a. 있을 법한, 있음직한
probably ad. 아마도, 대체로
probability n.가능성, 가망성, 확률
environmental a. 환경의, 보호의
environmentally ad. 환경적으로, 환경 보호적으로
environment n. 환경, 주위의 정황
environmentalist n. 환경론자, 환경 전문가

original a. 독창적인; 본래의
originally ad. 원래는, 본래는
originality n. 독창성, 창의
originator n.창작자
origin n. 기원

intended a. 의도된, 고의의
intention n. 계획, 목적, 의도
intending a. 지망하는
intentional a. 고의적인

return v. 재 방문하다, 되돌아오다
n. 반송, 돌아옴
returning 되돌아오는
returned 되돌아 온

ideal a. 이상적인
ideality n. 이상적인 것, 상상력
ideally ad. 이상적으로,
idealize v. ~을 이상화하다
idealist n. 이상주의자

challenge n. 도전 v. 도전 하게하다
challenging a. 힘든, 도전적인

formal a. 공식적인
formally ad. 공식적으로
formality n. 공식, 인습
formalize v. 공식화하다

positive a. 긍정적인, 호의적인
positively ad. 긍정적으로
positivity n. 적극성; 확실함
positiveness n. 긍정적 태도

operate v. 운영하다, 경영하다
operational: a. (기계 따위가) 운전[운행] 가능한
operation: n. 운행
operationally: ad. 기능을 다하여, 운행 가능하게

favor n. 호의 v. 호의를 베풀다
favorable a. 좋은, 호의적인
favorably ad. 알맞게, 호의적으로

commerce n.상업, 무역
commercial a.상업적인; n.광고
commercially ad.상업적으로,
commercializing 상품화한, 상업화한

monitor v. 측정하다, 관찰하다,
monitoring n. 측정, 감시, 관찰

excellently ad. 우수하게
excellence n. 우수, 탁월성
excellent a. 훌륭한, 우수한

excite v. 흥분시키다
excitement n. 흥분
excited a. 흥분한 (사람수식)
exciting a. 흥분하는 (사물수식)

short a. 짧은
shorten v. 짧게 하다
shortly ad. 곧

reason n. 이유
reasonable a. 합리적인
reasonably ad. 합리적으로
reasoning n. 추론, 논리적 사고

arrival n.도착
arrive v. 도착하다
arrange v. 주선하다, 계획하다
arrangement n. 조정; 정돈, 배치

voluntary a. 자발적인
volunteer n. 자원 봉사자, 지원자
v. 자원하다, 자청하다
voluntarily ad. 자발적으로, 스스로

skillful a. ~를 잘하는
skillfully ad. 솜씨 있게
skilled a. 숙련된, 노련한
skills n. 기술, 숙련

significance n. 중요, 중요성
significant a. 중요한
significantly ad. 두드러 지게
signification n. 의미, 의의

★ approximately ad. 대략
approximate v. ~에 가까워지다
approximation n. 접근

state v. 진술하다
n. 상태
stated a. 진술된; 정해진, 정기의
statement n. 성명(서), 진술

application n. 지원
applicant n. 지원자
apply v. 지원하다
apply for ~에 지원하다

mistaken a. 틀린, 오해한
mistakable a. 틀리기 쉬운
mistakenly ad. 실수로, 잘못하여
mistake n. 잘못; 틀리다, 오해하다
make a mistake 실수하다

interaction n. 상호 작용
interactive a. 상호 작용하는
interact v. 상호 작용하다

bright a. 밝은
brighten v. 밝게 하다
brightly ad. 밝게

high a. 높은 ad. 높게
highly ad. 매우

professional n. 전문가(사람도 됨!!)
a. 전문적인
profession n. (전문적인) 직업
professionally ad. 전문적으로

proposal n. 제안
propose v. 제안하다

follow v. 따르다
following 전. ~에 이어, ~후에
= after a. 다음의

adequacy n. 충분함 (명사어휘 거의 쓰이지 않음)
adequateness n. 적당함
(명사어휘 거의 쓰이지 않음)
adequately ad. 충분히, 적당하게
adequate a. 충분한, 적당한

serve v. ~을 위하여 일하다
service n. 근무, 복역
server n. 웨이터나 웨이트리스

medical a. 의학의; 치료용의
medicate v. 약으로 치료하다
medicine n. 약
medicinal a. 약의, 약효가 있는

extent n. 넓이; 범위
extend v. 뻗다; 연장하다
extensive a. 광범위한, (지식이) 해박한

compare v. 비교하다
comparable a. 동일한, 동등한; 비교할 수 있는
comparison n. 비교
comparatively ad. 비교적, 상당히

rely on v. 신뢰하다
reliant on a. ~ 의지하는
reliance n. 신뢰, 신임
reliable a. 믿을 수 있는, 신뢰할 수 있는

expired a. 유효하지 않은, 만기가 된
expiration n. (기간·임기 등의) 만료, 만기
expire: v. 만기 되다

stronger a. 더 강한
strengthen v. 강화하다, 강하게 만들다
strong a. 강한
strength n. 힘

recognize v. 인정하다
recognized a. 인정 받는
recognizing a. 인정하는

select v. 선택하다
selected a. 선택된
selection n. 선택
selective a. 선택적인

familiarity: n. 친밀, 친근
familiarize: v. ~을 친숙하게 하다
familiar: a. 낯익은
familiarly: ad. 친근하게

publish: v. 출판하다
publication: n. 출판, 출판물
publisher: n. 출판사 , 출판업자

celebration: n. 축하, 기념
celebrate: v. 축하하다
celebrated: a. 유명한, 저명한
in celebration of ~를 축하하여

vary: v. 다양하게 하다; 바꾸다
various: a. 다양한
variety: n. 다양(성)
variously: ad 다양하게

afford: v. ~할 여유가 있다
affordable: a. 입수 가능한, 알맞은
affordably: ad. 입수할 수 있게

severity: n. 엄격, 가혹
severely: ad. 심하게, 엄격하게
severe: a. 심한, 격심한

accorded: a. 일치된
according : ad. ~에 따라서
according to 로 사용함 ~에 따라서
accordingly: ad. 따라서, 그래서,
accordance: n. 일치, 조화

treat: v. 치료하다
treatment: n. 치료

determine: v. 결정하다
determiner: n. 결정하는 사람
determined a. 확고한

part: n. 부분; 부속
partly: ad. 어느정도는; 부분적으로

conclude: v. 끝내다, 종결하다
conclusion: n. 결론
conclusive: a. 확정적인
concluding: a. 종결의, 최후의

enclosed: a. 동봉된
enclosure: n. 동봉(한 것), 동봉물
enclose: v. 동봉하다
enclosing: a. 동봉하는

preparation: n. 준비
prepare: v. 준비하다
preparatory: a. 준비의
in preparation for ~을 준비하여, ~을 대비하여

understandable: a. 이해할 수 있는,
understandably: ad. 이해할 수 있게
understanding: a. 이해력 있는
understand: v. 이해하다

permit: v. 허락하다
permissive: a. 허용된, 허락하는
permission: n. 허락
permitted: a. 허락된

be permitted toV ~하는 것이 허락되다

removal: n. 처분, 제거
removable: a. 제거 가능한
removed: a. 제거된
remover: n. 제거자

inspect: v. 점검하다; 시찰하다
inspector: n. 조사관, 검사자
inspection: n. 검사; 시찰

great: a. 큰, 거대한
ad. 훌륭하게
greatest 가장 큰 (great 의 최상급)
greatly: ad. 매우, 크게

grateful: a. 고맙게 여기는, 감사하는

locate: v. 위치를 정하다, (위치 등을) 찾아내다
locally: ad. 장소상으로
location: n. 장소, 위치
locality: n. 소재, 근처

manage: v. 경영하다; 다루다; 이럭저럭 해내다
manager: n. 경영자, 관리자, 지배인
managerial: a. 관리의, 지배인

representative: n. 대표자
representational: a. 대표하는
represent: v. 대표하다

impression: n. 인상, 감명
impressive: a. 대규모의, 장엄한;
impressively: ad. 인상적으로
impressiveness: n. 인상 깊음

dramatize: v. 각색하다; 과장하다
dramatist: n. 극작가, 희곡 작가
dramatic: a. 극의; 각본의;
dramatically: ad. 극적으로; 인상적으로

fund: n. 자금
v. 자금을 대다
funding: n. 자금 지원

preventability: n. 예방할 수 있음
prevention: n. 예방, 저지
preventable: a. 예방할 수 있는

athlete: n. 운동 선수, 경기자
athletic: a. 활발한, 운동경기의,
athletics: n. 체육학, 운동경기

compliment: n. 찬사, 칭찬의 말;
complimentary: a.무료의, 칭찬하는

exclusion: n. 제외, 배척, 추방
exclusionary: a. 배제의, 제외의
exclusively: ad. 오로지(~만); 독점적으로; 배타적으로
exclusiveness: n. 배타성, 독점성, 유일성

extreme: a. 극도의, 극심한; 극단적인 것
extremity: n. 끝, 말단
extremely: ad. 대단히, 극도로, 극단적으로

comfortableness: n. 쾌적함; 안락함
comfort: v. 위안하다; 위안, 위로
comfort: n. 위로, 위안; 안심.
comfortable: a. 안락한; 편안한
comfortably: ad. 편안하게

manufacture: v. 제조하다
manufacturer: n. 제조업자

prompt: a. 재빠른, 신속한
prompter: n. <연극> (배우의) 후견역
promptly: ad. 정각에, 즉시

initial: a. 초기의, 최초의
initiate: v. 시작하다
initiation: n. 착수
initially: ad. 처음에

motive: n. 동기, 자극
motivate: v. ~에게 동기를 주다
motivation: n. 열의; 동기 부여
motivational: a. 동기 부여의

appoint: v. 임명하다, 지명하다
appointed: a. 임명된
appointment: n. 임명, 지명

charity: n. 자비심; 자선
charitably: ad. 자비롭게, 관대하게
charitableness: n. 자비로움, 관대함

performance: n. 실적, 성과: 수행
perform: v. 실행하다, 수행하다

finance: v. 자금을 조달하다
n. 자금
financial: a. 재정상의, 재무의
financially: ad. 재정적으로, 재정상

occasion: n. (특정한) 때, 경우
occasional: a. 가끔, 때때로의
occasionally: ad. 때때로

dining: n. 식사, 정찬
dine: v. ~와 식사를 하다

viewer: n. 관찰자, 구경꾼
viewable: a. 볼 수 있는
view: n. 의견, 견해, 생각

dignity: n. 존엄, 위엄, 품위
dignify: v. 위엄 있게 하다
dignified: a. 기품 있는

regulate: v. 통제하다
regulator: n. 통제자
regulation: n. 규칙, 규정

accomplish: v. 성취하다, 달성하다
accomplishment: n. 업적, 성취
admission: n. 입학
admit: v. 입학을 허가하다; 인정하다

responsive: a. 응답하는, 반응하는
response: n. 반응, 응답
respond: v. 응답하다
respond to ~응답하다

conductor: n. 안내자; 지휘자
conduct: v. 행동하다; 이끌다, 안내하다

impossible: a. 불가능한
impossibly: ad. 불가능하게
impossibility: n. 불가능한 일

technical: a. 기술적인
technicality: n. 학술적임
technology: n. 기술
technician: n. 기술자

extended: a. 연장한; 광범위에 걸친
extendable: a. 넓힐 수 있는
extend: v. 연장하다; 넓히다
extension: n. 연장; 확장

satisfy: v. 만족시키다
satisfactory: a. 만족스러운
satisfaction: n. 만족
satisfactorily: ad. 만족하게
be satisfied with ~만족스러운

knowledge: n. 지식
knowledgeable (about): a. 많이 아는
knowingly: ad. 일부러, 고의로

distraction: n. 산만하게 하는 것
distract: v. (마음을) 어지럽히다
distracting: a. 정신을 어지럽히는

competition: n. 경쟁
competitor: n. 경쟁자
competitive: a. 경쟁적인
compete: v. 경쟁하다

significantly: ad. 상당히
significant: a. 중대한, 주목할 만한
signify: v, ~의 뜻을 나타내다
significance: n. 의미

excessive: a. 과도한
excess: n. 과도함
excessively: ad. 과도하게

variety: n. 다양성
various: a. 다양한
variation: n. 변화, 변동
variably: ad. 변덕스럽게

resist: v. 반대하다; ~에 저항하다
resistance: 반대; 견딤, 저항
resistant: 견디는, 저항하는

fortunately: ad. 다행히도
fortunate: a. 운이 좋은, 행운의
fortune: n. 운; 부, 재산

appropriate: a. 적절한
appropriately: ad. 적절하게

compare: v. 비교하다, 대조하다
comparable: a. 비슷한, 비교할 수 있는

probable: a. 있을 법한, 있음직한
probably: ad. 아마도
probability: n. 가망성, 가능성

add: v. ~을 더하다, 추가하다
additional: a. 추가적인
addition: n. 추가
additionally: ad. 추가적으로

repeat: v. 되풀이하다, 반복하다
repeater: n. 되풀이하는 사람(것)
repetition: n. 되풀이, 반복
repeatedly: ad. 되풀이 하여

inform: v. 알리다, 통지하다
informer: n. 정보 제공자
information: n. 정보
informative: 유익한, 교육적인

maintain: v. 지속하다; 유지하다
maintenance: n. 유지, 보수 관리

exclusive: a. 배타적인
excluding: prep. 전치사 (= except) ~을 제외하고
exclusively: ad. 오로지, 전문적으로, 독점적으로, 배타적으로

support: n, 원조, 후원
support: v. 원조하다, 후원하다
supporter: n. 후원자, 지지자
supporting: a. 지지하는, 원조하는

conscience: n. 양심
conscientious: a. 양심적인, 성실한
conscientiousness: n. 양심적임, 성실함
conscientiously: ad. 양심적으로, 공들여

substance: n. 물질, 본질
substantial: a. 상당한
substantiate: v. ~을 증명하다, ~을 구체화하다

convenient: a. 편리한
conveniently: ad. 편리하게
convenience: n. 편리, 편의

reform: n. 개혁
reformer: n. 개혁가
reformatory: a. 개혁의, 혁신적인

motivate: v. 자극하다, ~에게 동기를 주다
motivator: n. 자극자, 동기부여자

suggest: v. 제안하다
suggestion: n. 제안

propose: v. 제안하다
proposal: n. 제안, 제안서

periodic: a. 주기적인, 정기적인
periodical: n. 정기 간행물
a. 정기 간행물의
period: n. 기간
periodically: ad. 정기적으로

spacing: n. 간격을 띄움, 공간적 배치
spacious: a. 넓은
spaciousness: n. 넓음, 거대함
space: n. 공간

advisable: a. 현명한
advisor: n. 조언자
advice: n. 충고, 조언

addition: n. 추가, 부가
additional: a. 추가적인
additionally: ad. 부가적으로

visit: v. 방문하다
visitor: n. 방문객
visitation: n. 방문

amaze: v. 몹시 놀라게 하다
amazement: n. 놀람
amazingly: ad. 놀랄 만하게 , 굉장하게
amazing: a. 놀랄 만한, 굉장한

predictable: a. 예측 할 수 있는
predictably: ad. 예측 할 수 있게
predict: v. 예측하다

establish: v. (제도. 법률 등을) 제정하다
established: a. 확정된, 확립된

regular: a. 정기적인
regularly: ad. 정기적으로
regularity: n. 규칙 바름, 일정불변
regulate: v. ~을 규제하다

제3강

문장의 구조와 성분

▌문장을 구성하는 성분 / 역할 / 위치

순서	성분	각 성분이 하는일	성분의 위치 / 품사
1	주어 (Subject)	동작의 주체	동사 앞에 있는 **명사**
2	동사 (Verb)	주어의 동작, 상태	문장에서 **기준**
3	목적어 (Object) 대상어	주어가 하는 동작의 대상	동사 뒤에 있는 **명사**
4	보어 (Complement)	주어, 목적어를 보충설명	Be 동사 뒤 **명사나 형용사** 목적어 뒤 **명사나 형용사**

▌다음 기초 문장들을 분석해봅시다.

The CEO resigned.

Registration begins at 7 A.M.

The cost of housing rose dramatically last year.

His qualifications are impressive, so he is likely to get hired.

They were my coworkers.

Participants should submit their evaluations of this new hair dryer.

Many employees submitted complain about the long working hours.

출제 포인트

Q1. [주어 자리] + 동사

The ___________ about the new software was successful.

(A) presents (B) presenter

(C) presented (D) presentation

★ 설명 : 주어자리에는 항상 명사가 들어갑니다. 앞에서 배운 품사를 구분하는 방법을 기억해서 명사를 찾아내는 연습! 명사외에도 대명사, 동명사, to부정사, 명사절이 주어 자리에 들어갈 수 있습니다.

Q2. 명사 + [동사 자리]

The concert ________________ with a performance by a famous singer.

(A) concluding (B) to conclude

(C) concluded (D) conclusion

★ 설명 : 동사자리에는 to / ing 가 붙은 동사는 들어갈 수 없습니다. 명령문은 주어 없이 동사원형으로 시작할 수 있습니다.

Q3. 동사 + [목적어 자리]

We offer free ________________ if your order is more that $50.

(A) deliver (B) delivery

(C) deliverable (D) delivers

★ 설명 : 목적어 자리에는 항상 명사가 들어갑니다. 앞에서 배운 품사를 구분하는 방법을 기억해서 명사를 찾아야합니다. 명사외에도 대명사, 동명사, to부정사, 명사절이 목적어 자리에 들어갈 수 있습니다.

Q4. 동사 + 명사 + [보어 자리]

The seminar attendees found his speech ________________.

(A) impressive
(B) impressively
(C) impress
(D) impression

★ 설명 : 보어자리에는 명사나 형용사가 들어갑니다.

품사 실전문제

1. Workers at the factory are too ______.
   (A) busyness (B) is busy
   (C) busily (D) busy

2. RED company ______ its workforce by 20 percent this year.
   (A) will increase (B) increasing
   (C) to increase (D) being increased

3. The responses from the customer survey are ______ positive.
   (A) consistency (B) consistencies
   (C) consistently (D) consistent

4. You can renew ______ to Beauty Updates Magazine online or by telephone.
   (A) subscribers (B) subscribes
   (C) subscriptions (D) subscribe

5. The ______ of Jay Factory to East lansing will occur in April.
   (A) relocate (B) relocated
   (C) relocation (D) relocates

6. Because the sofa is very ______, at least two people have to move it.
   (A) heavily (B) heavy
   (C) heaviness (D) most heavily

7. ______ at the factory usually receive a salary at the end of the month.
   (A) Work (B) Workers
   (C) Working (D) Works

8. The salad dressing is ______.

(A) sweetness (B) sweet

(C) sweeten (D) sweetly

9. We ______ the office complex in a suburb of the city.

(A) will build (B) to build

(C) building (D) builder

10. ______ of this task is not expected until April

(A) Completed (B) Completely

(C) Completion (D) Completes

제4강

문장을 결정하는 중요 동사들

1. 주어 + go, come, work, depart, run, fall + 쓰레기(부사/전명구)

Unemployment fell.

Unemployment fell sharply.

Unemployment fell in December.

2. 주어 + be, become, remain, stay(유지하다) + 주격보어(형용사만)

The prices are reasonable.

My supervisor became a general manager.

3. 주어 + 대부분의 동사들 + 목적어 (명사)

The company expanded the services.

They inspect the factory.

4. 주어 + give, send, show, teach, tell, offer, grant + 목적어(명사) + 목적어(명사)

▲ 수동태의 경우 : be + pp + 명사 가능 (해석을 병행) - 수동태 편에서 추가설명

The store will give customers a discount.

The company grants employees bonuses.

We can send you the product within a week.

5. 주어 + make, keep, find, think, consider + 목적어(명사) + 목적격보어(형용사)

▲ 수동태의 경우 : be + pp + 형용사

I found their benefits package attractive.

We consider his opinion interesting.

5-1. 주어 + call, name, elect + 목적어(명사) + 목적격보어(명사) -(직업이 쓰임)

▲ 수동태의 경우 : be + pp + 명사 (직책, 직업)

We elected Mr. Kim the presient.

5-2. 주어 + make, have, let (사역동사) + 목적어(명사) + 목적격보어(동사원형)
주어 + help(준사역동사) + 목적어(명사) + 목적격보어(동사원형/to부정사)

I have my secretary send an important E-mail.

Yoga will help you relieve / to relieve stress.

5-3. 주어 + 설득/허락/기대/권고 + 목적어(명사) + 목적격보어(to부정사)

▲ 수동태의 경우 : be + pp + to동사원형

설득: persuade, convince, encourage, motivate, compel, force, tell, teach

허락: permit, allow, enable

기대: expect, want, would like, require

권고: cause, remind, invite, advise, ask, urge

They asked applicants to submit resumes by mail.

My co-worker advised me to open a new branch.

The machine can enable them to create more products.

5-4. 주어 + ANICAR 동사 + 목적어(명사) + of 명사/to 동원/that what +문장

▲ 수동태의 경우 : be + pp + to+동원/of+명사/that, what+주어+동사

Assure / Notify / Inform / Convince / Advise / Remind 삼성화재 애니카!

The flight attendant remind passengers to fasten their seat belt.
The president informed employees of the change in the payroll system.

이 부분은 무조건 외워야합니다. 외우면 편해집니다.

문장을 결정하는 중요 동사 Quiz

1. 주어 + ______________________ + 쓰레기(부사/전명구)

2. 주어 + ______________________ + 형용사

3. 주어 + _____________ + 명사1

4. 주어 + ______________________ + 명사1 + 명사2

5. 주어 + ______________________ + 명사1 + 형용사1
   be + pp + 형용사

5-1. 주어 + ________________ + 명사1 + 동사원형 – 사역동사
   ~하게 만들다, 시키다, 허락하다
   주어 + ________ (준사역동사) + 명사1 + 동사원형/to+동사원형

5-2. 주어 + ____________ + 명사1 + 명사2(직책, 직업)
   선출하다, 부르다, 임명하다

5-3. 주어 + 설득/허락/기대/권고 + 명사1 + to 동사원형

설득: ______________________________
   설득하다, 설득하다, 권고하다, 동기부여하다. 꾸짖다, 강제로~하게하다, 말하다 가르치다

허락: ______________________________
   인정하다, 허락하다, ~할 수 있게하다

기대: ______________________________
   기대하다, 원하다, ~하고싶다, 요구하다

권고: ______________________________
   ~의 원인이다, 상기시키디, 권고하다, 조언하다, 요청하다, 촉구하다

5-4. 주어 + ANICAR 동사 + 명사1 + of 명사/to 동원/that what + 주어+동사
   be + pp + to+동원/of+명사/that, what+주어+동사

   ____

   확신시키다, 알리다, 알리다, 설득하다, 조언하다, 상기시키다

동사 실전문제

1. The varying quality of products can make purchase decisions quite ______.
(A) difficulties (B) difficulty
(C) difficultly (D) difficult

2. The government's new employement policy will enable business ______ many jobs.
(A) to create (B) creating
(C) created (D) create

3. The president informed employees of the ______ in the payroll system.
(A) to change (B) changing
(C) changed (D) change

4. The Marketing Department encouraged employees ______ their feedback reports as soon as possible.
(A) to submit (B) submitting
(C) submitted (D) submit

5. Every team member should work ______ on this project.
(A) collaborative (B) collaboratively
(C) collaborates (D) collaborator

6. Moonfield Shopping Center reminded customers ______ their business hours will change from March 1.
(A) to (B) that
(C) of (D) for

7. Researchers found the recycling system ______ in reducing garbage.
(A) effect (B) effects
(C) effective (D) effectively

8. The personnel manager helps new employees ______ knowledgeable about the new system.(답2개)

(A) became (B) becoming

(C) become (D) to become

9. The HR director advised employees ______ for the workshop ahead of time.

(A) register (B) to register

(C) be registered (D) registering

10. The manager will have his assistant ______ the proceedings of the meeting.

(A) transcribe (B) to be transcribed

(C) be transcribing (D) transcribed

제5강

동사 – 수의 일치

1. 수 일치의 기본

문장의 주어인 명사는 단수와 복수가 있다. 주어에 따라 동사의 형태가 달라진다.

○ 단수주어 + 단수동사

○ 주어가 단수일 경우 be동사는 is/was, 일반동사는 -s, -es를 붙인다.

The red light **flashes** to show low battery power.

All equipment **is** on sale with a 30% discount in October.

○ 복수주어 + 복수동사

○ 주어가 복수일 경우 be 동사는 are/were, 일반동사는 원형 그대로 쓴다.

The employees **take** responsibility for quality control in this facility.

An inspector and an executive **visit** the factory every month.

2. 수 일치의 패턴

○ 주어 + (수식어) + 동사 – 주어와 동사사이에 수식어가 들어간 경우

The products of the company **are** good.

The company producing computers **has** a good reputation

The customers who used our rental service **were** satisfied.

○ 수량표현 of 복수명사

○ Most, all, half, rest, some, any of + 단/복수 + 단/복수 동사를 쓴다.

Most of the information **is** available free of charge.

Half of the employees **want** to stay for next five years.

○ Each/Every 패턴 - 항상 뒤에 단수명사를 쓰고, 단수동사를 쓴다

Every employee attends the meeting evey morning.

○ A number of (많은) + 복수명사 + 복수동사

○ The number of (~의 수) + 복수명사 + 단수동사

A number of students are studying.

The number of students is going to increase.

수의 일치 실전문제

1. Nearly 500 people from all over the country ______ for the annual conference on environmental studies.
   (A) is registering (B) has registered
   (C) registers (D) register

2. The final installment in the popular mystery series ______ due to arrive in tores yesterday, but unexpected shipping problems caused delays.
   (A) was (B) were
   (C) is (D) are

3. The monthly training programs ________ employees skills that make them more efficient.
   (A) teach (B) is teaching
   (C) has taught (D) be taught

4. The policy on vacation days ______ to both full-time and part-time workers.
   (A) application (B) applies
   (C) apply (D) applying

5. The number of employees of the company ______ by 10% this year.
   (A) are increasing (B) has increased
   (C) were increased (D) have been increased

6. Every employee ______ to consider what his or her prospects are for career advancement.
   (A) have needed (B) needs
   (C) needing (D) to need

7. The waitress recommended the steak dish which ______ with potatoes.
   (A) come (B) to come
   (C) coming (D) comes

8. Some of the defective products ______ going to be shipped to JA warehouses.
(A) was (B) to be
(C) be (D) are

9. Please complete the feedback form before you ______ the room.
(A) to leave (B) had left
(C) leaving (D) leave

10. The recent decline in retail sales ______ been blamed on the tax increses.
(A) has (B) have
(C) having (D) to have

11. There ______ many boxes at the lobby of the hotel yesterday.
(A) was (B) to be
(C) be (D) are

12. The customer ______ a bottle of shampoo yesterday.
(A) purchasing (B) purchased
(C) to purchase (D) purchase

13. One of the candidates ______ some misleading information in the resume.
(A) including (B) included
(C) include (D) to be included

14. The orders typically _____ four days to process.
(A) takes (B) taking
(C) take (D) to take

15. Please _____ the manual carefully before installing your new word processing software.
(A) reading (B) read
(C) to read (D) reads

16. She _____ a donation to the community.
(A) have made (B) has made
(C) having made (D) making

17. Ms. Rares _____ more information about the workshop.
(A) needs (B) needing
(C) need (D) to need

18. You can easily _____ East Manhattan by taking the Yellow Rail Line.
(A) reaches (B) reach
(C) to reach (D) reacing

19. The _____ of our vehicle is going to increase.
(A) productivity (B) productive
(C) productivities (D) produce

20. Mr. Kim, the office manager, always _____ new menu.
(A) develops (B) develop
(C) to develop (D) development

제6강

동사 – 시제

1. 시제 문제 해결의 기본

시간을 알려주는 힌트들을 빠르게 찾는 것이 관건!

2. 시제의 구성

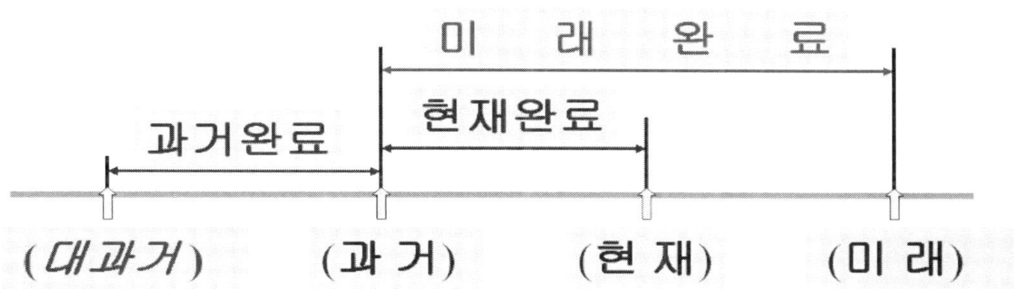

○ 현재 시제를 알려주는 힌트들

+

usually/generally 보통	often/frequently 자주	regularly 정기적으로
sometimes 때때로	always 늘	every/each 매번
daily 매일	monthly 매달	yearly 매년

Every week, several flights _____ round trips from Seoul to Hong Kong.

(A) make (B) making

(C) makes (D) has made

○ 과거 시제를 알려주는 힌트들

시간 + ago ~전	last + 시간 지난~	in + 지난연도/세기 ~에
recently/lately 최근에	once 한때	yesterday 어제
then 그때에	previously 이전에	those days 그 당시에
at one time 한때는, 과거에는	at that time 그 때	

Samsung Finace _____ a sports center in the office facilities **two month ago**.

(A) building (B) built

(C) has built (D) builds

○ 미래 시제를 알려주는 힌트들

tomorrow 내일	next + 시간 다음 ~에
starting/beginning + 미래 시점 ~부터	as of + 미래시점 ~부로
in the near/foreseeable future 가까운 미래에	soon/shortly 곧
this coming / upcoming 다가오는	by/until ~까지
at this time + 미래 시점 ~할 때에	by the time ~할 때까지

Some analysts predic that the worldwide market _____ by 75% in the **next decade**.

(A) be grown (B) growing

(C) has grown (D) will grow

○ 현재완료 시제(have/has p.p)

recently/lately 최근에			for/over/during the past/last + 기간 지난~동안	
since ~ 이후로	just 막	yet 아직 (부정문)	already 이미	in ~ 동안

완료 용법 : 과거에 이미 완료된 일

Amery & Co. has just released their new line of footwear in New York.

경험 용법 : "~해본 적이 있다/없다" 등 경험의 유무
The workers have recently visited the Agriculture Museum to learn about farming.

계속 용법 : "~해오고 있다" 등 과거에 발생하여 현재까지 이어지는 일 - 가장 자주 사용
Hank's Office Supply Inc. has been in business since 1974.

결과 용법 : "~했다" 등 과거에 발생하여 그 결과가 현재까지 영향을 미치는 일
Mr. Singh has lost his rental agreement, so we should print out a new one.

○ 과거완료 시제(had p.p) : 기준이 되는 과거 제시, 그보다 더 과거를 나타날 때
Vernard Clothing Mart had operated for 40 years before it closed down last week.

○ 미래완료 시제(will have p.p) : 과거부터의 일이 미래까지 계속되어 완료되는 일
At the end of this year, the construction company will have completed the project.

※ 시제 일치 예외 : 시간/조건 접속사가 이끄는 부사절 안에서는 현재가 미래를 대신한다.

시간	when / by the time / as ~할 때 as soon as ~하자마자 while ~하는 동안	before ~ 전에 since ~ 이래로 until ~할 때까지	after ~ 후에
조건	if / provided (that) / providing (that) ~이라면 unless / if not 만약 ~이 아니라면 once 일단 ~하면	 as long as / as far as ~하는 한 in case ~하는 경우에는	

The manager will call us when he **gets** to the construction site **tomorrow**.

○ 당위성 동사나 판단의 형용사 뒤에 오는 that 절에는 'should + 동사원형'을 쓴다.

당위성 동사	suggest/recommend/propose 제안하다		
	insist/urge 주장하다		order/command 명령하다
	demand/request/ask/require 요구하다, 요청하다		advise 충고하다
당위성 형용사	necessary 필요한	important 중요한	desirable 바람직한
	imperative 긴급한, 필수의	essential 필수의	vital 필수의

MS. Suh suggest that the empty office (should) **be** turned into a staff fitness center.

It is essential that we (should) **do** best to make our customers satisfied with our work.

시제 실전문제

1. By next fall, the metro Art Museum _____ both local and national artists.
   (A) exhibit (B) exhibited
   (C) exhibiting (D) will exhibit

2. Due to additional funding, the traffic lights on Preston Street have _____ been upgraded.
   (A) early (B) yet
   (C) already (D) ever

3. Over the next couple of weeks, the Festival Theather _____ auditions for its newest play.
   (A) held (B) has held
   (C) will hold (D) had been holding

4. The company will _____ expand its manufacturing facilities in Detroit.
   (A) frequently (B) recently
   (C) soon (D) regularly

5. Liza Baley _____ received positive reviews for her performance.
   (A) formally (B) regularly
   (C) recently (D) soon

6. We have seen a number of changes in the way we do business since the new president _____ in.
   (A) come (B) comes
   (C) came (D) is coming

7. Customers usually _____ to Sado's Diner due to its excellent service and delicious food.
   (A) return (B) has returned
   (C) returns (D) have been returned

8. Since Ms. Pham joined the company, sales _____ amlost by 30 percent.
   (A) increased (B) had increased
   (C) have increased (D) will have increased

9. Yannick has been involved in 4-H for eight years and has been President ______ over 3 years.
(A) in (B) for
(C) up (D) from

10. Dishes and silverware are __________ stored in cabinets near eating area or dishwasher for easy access.
(A) relatively (B) slightly
(C) usually (D) vaguely

11. Over the past decade, LG Electronics _____________ a wide range of high-definition TV.
(A) selling (B) to sell
(C) has sold (D) will be selling

12. Ms. Reddy _____________ operations of the new factory when it opens next April.
(A) had overseen (B) oversaw
(C) will oversee (D) overseeing

13. Baprix Industries will __________ expand its manufacturing facilities in Detroit.
(A) usually (B) recently
(C) soon (D) formerly

14. Staring nest Wednesday, the Vianox Shopping Center _______________ its business hours until 10 P.M.
(A) was extending (B) had extended
(C) are extending (D) will be extending

15. Both Ms. Li and Ms. Chau _______________ at Wantari group for over seven years.
(A) work (B) will be working
(C) works (D) have worked

16. Once the director ___________ the renovation projects on Wednesday, the contractor will start the interior early next week.
(A) approves (B) approval
(C) approvable (D) approvingly

17. Security system at Wilmington has greatly improved since the revised safety procedures ____________ implemented.

(A) were
(B) to be
(C) will be
(D) been

18. Last week's meeting ____________ opportunities for new employees to learn ideas and meet new people.

(A) creating
(B) creates
(C) created
(D) will create

19. ________ the past ten years, the number of speed-related car accidents has gone up by 10%.

(A) Over
(B) On
(C) At
(D) Of

20. Kirks Departments Store ____________ open for over 20 years.

(A) have been
(B) has been
(C) is
(D) to be

제7강

동사 – 능동태와 수동태

1. 수동태 기본

동사 뒤 목적어가 있으면 능동태

The company holds **the event** every December.
동사 목적어

The company recommended **Jason** for the manager position.
동사 목적어

동사 뒤 목적어가 없으면 수동태

The event **is held** every December.
be +p.p(과거분사)

Jason was **recommended** for the manager position.
be +p.p(과거분사)

주어가 행위를 능동적으로 하면 능동태, 행위의 대상이 되면 수동태

○ 자동사(1형식, 2형식)는 수동태로 쓸 수 없다(목적어가 없어도 항상 능동태).

1형식	rise 오르다 proceed 진행하다	work 일하다	arrive 도착하다 occur / take place 일어나다
2형식	be동사 ~이 되다 remain/stay/keep ~상태를 유지하다 look/appear ~으로 보이다		become ~이 되다 seem ~인 듯하다 feel ~이라고 느끼다

○ '자동사 + 전치사'는 뒤에 목적어를 취할 수 있으므로 수동태로 쓸 수 있다.

account for	설명하다	be accounted for
carry out	실행하다	be carried out
deal with	다루다, 해결하다	be dealt with
take care of	돌보다, 담당하다	be taken care of
rely on	의존하다	be relied on
refer to	언급하다	be referred to
interfere with	방해하다	be interfered with

Ms. Lim will **take care of** planning next week's work schedules.

→ Planning next week's work schedules will **be taken care of** by Ms. Lim.

○ 목적어를 두 개 취하는 수여동사(4형식)는 수동태 뒤에 목적어가 올 수 있다.

4형식의 능동태 형태 : 주어 + 동사 + 목적어1 + 목적어2

4형식의 수동태 형태 : 주어 + be+p.p + 목적어2

give 주다	offer 제공하다	send 보내다, 파견하다
grant 주다, 부여하다		bring 가져오다
award (상을)수여하다, 보답하다		show 보여주다
lend 빌려주다		pay 지불하다

We **gave** Mr. Woodson the agenda for Tuesday's meeting.

→ Mr. Woodson **was given** the agenda for Tuesday's meeting.

○ 형용사를 목적격 보어로 갖는 5형식 동사는 수동태 뒤에 형용사가 온다.

5형식의 능동태 : 주어 + 동사 + 목적어 + 형용사

5형식의 수동태 : 주어 + be+p.p + 형용사

make 만들다	keep 유지하다	find 알게 되다
think 생각하다	consider 여기다	

The workers consider the safety management system **adequate**.

→ The safety management system is considered **adequate** by the workers.

○ **to+동사원형(to부정사)을 목적격 보어로 갖는 5형식의 동사는 수동태 뒤에 to+동원 이 온다.**

5형식의 능동태 : 주어 + 동사 + 목적어 + to+동사원형

5형식의 수동태 : 주어 + be+p.p + to+동사원형

be asked/invited/requested/required toV ~하도록 요청받다	
be allowed/permitted toV ~하도록 허락되다	be encouraged toV ~하도록 장려되다
be expected toV ~하도록 예정되다/기대되다	be advised toV ~하도록 권고되다
be forced toV ~하도록 강요받다	be instructed toV ~하도록 지시받다

The landlord asked the tenants **to pay** their rents.
동사 목적어 목적격보어

→ The tenants were asked **to pay** their rents (by the landlord).
be+p.p 목적격보어

수동태 실전문제

1. The construction crews _________ the project on schedule.
   (A) finished (B) are finished
   (C) finishing (D) to be finished

2. A large apartment complex _________ next to the Barhill train station.
   (A) will be built (B) builder
   (C) built (D) build

3. All images in the magazine have been _________ provided by the SE Association.
   (A) generousness (B) generosity
   (C) generously (D) generous

4. The weekly sales meeting is usually _________ in the morning.
   (A) conducted (B) conducts
   (C) conductor (D) conducting

5. Furiko Corporation _________ financial problems for several years.
   (A) has faced (B) has been faced
   (C) have faced (D) face

6. Ms. Silva is very _________ in attending the marketing seminar next week.
   (A) interested (B) interest
   (C) interesting (D) interests

7. Bromville Apartments' heating system _________ by the proprety management office this morning.
   (A) inspector (B) is being inspected
   (C) was inspecting (D) inspection

8. All team members can apply for a bonus once they _________ here for one year.
   (A) have worked (B) have been worked
   (C) are working (D) work

9. Mr. Hassan will ___________ all hotel reservations while Ms. Yang is away.
(A) handling (B) handle
(C) be handled (D) is handling

10. Applicants interested in the position ___________ to submit their resumes by November 30.
(A) require (B) requires
(C) are required (D) has required

11. Any requrest for a vacation must be ___________ to the supervision at least one week in advance.
(A) submitted (B) submission
(C) submit (D) submitting

12. All new employees should ___________ an orientation by the end of March.
(A) give (B) be given
(C) giving (D) be giving

13. Once next year's budget ___________, department heads can make their final decisions about allocation.
(A) has been approved (B) approves
(C) will approve (D) approved

14. Technicians are ___________ to wear safety helmets at all times while working in the plant.
(A) inquired (B) insisted
(C) appealed (D) requied

15. Business class seats are ___________ with Internet hook-ups and global telephones for all of your business needs.
(A) equip (B) equipment
(C) equipped (D) equipping

16. Mr. Greg ___________ to deliver a presentation at the monthly business workshop, but he declined the invitation.
(A) encouraged (B) has encouraged
(C) was encouraged (D) was encouraging

17. Customers are advised __________ this medicine in a cool, dry place after unsealing the bottle and not to take it more than twice a day.

(A) store
(B) storing
(C) stores
(D) to store

18. While Peach Street's parking lot _____________, visitors are strongly encouraged to use public transportation.

(A) repairs
(B) is being repaired
(C) have repaired
(D) repair

19. Until the new parts ________________ in the photocopier, please insert the copy paper very gently.

(A) were installing
(B) would be installing
(C) have installed
(D) have been installed

20. All the residents who are __________ about the proposed water rate increase will be invited to a public hearing next month.

(A) concerns
(B) concerned
(C) concerning
(D) concern

제8강

가정법

1. 가정법

- If를 주로 사용하는 문장이며, 동사의 시제를 정확히 구분해야한다.

○ 가정법 미래(현재시제사용) : 만약 ~하면, …할 것이다/하라

If + 주어 + 동사현재시제 ~, 주어 + will/can/may + 동사원형 or 명령믄
If + 주어 + should + 동사원형 ~, 주어 + will/can/may + 동사원형 or 명령문

If you **have** further questions, you **can feel** free to ask me at any time.
If you **should have** further questions, **please feel** free to ask me at any time.

○ 가정법 과거(과거시제사용) : 만약 ~한다면, …할 텐데 (현재 사실과 반대되는 상황)

If + 주어 + 동사의 과거형 ~, 주어 + would/should/could/might + 동사원형
우 슈 쿠 마 - 기억!

If Mr. Lewis **notified** us earlier, we **would have** enough time to prepare.

○ 가정법 과거완료 : 만약 ~했다면, …했을 텐데 (과거 사실과 반대되는 상황)

If + 주어 + had p.p ~, 주어 + would/should/could/might + have p.p

If we **had taken** the earlier flight, we **would have gotten** to the convention on time.

ㅇ 가정법 도치

가정법 구문에서 if를 생략하며 주어와 동사의 위치가 바뀌게 된다, 도치만 보고 가정법임을 판단 할수 있어야한다.

If it should rain tomorrow, please call me. → **Should** it rain tomorrow, please call me

If I were you, I would call him now. → **Were** I you, I would call him now.

If we had taken your advice, we would have saved a lot of time. → **Had** we taken ~

가정법 실전문제

1. If the theater decreased its prices, more customers ______________ to purchase a ticket.
(A) will afford
(B) afforded
(C) could afford
(D) have afforded

2. If the firm formed a partnership with the solar panel company, it ______________ research in renewable energy technology.
(A) would support
(B) having supported
(C) supported
(D) supports

3. If the warning light __________________ to flash, you will have to reset the digital camera.
(A) had continued
(B) continuing
(C) will continuing
(D) continues

4. I the machine _____ capable of producing more units per hour, we might install it in our factory.
(A) be
(B) were
(C) is
(D) been

5. If we had spent more time designing the packaging, we _________ higher sales now.
(A) are having
(B) having
(C) have had
(D) might have

6. If Ms. Etherington had not made the payment on June 30, ownership of the vehicle __________ to the original seller.
(A) will revrt
(B) being reverted
(C) has reverted
(D) would have reverted

7. If you ____________ to end your magazine subscription early, send an e-mail to our customer service department.
(A) had wished
(B) have wished
(C) should wish
(D) wished

8. Were there a better selection of clothing, we __________ at this store more often.
(A) would shop (B) shopped
(C) are shopping (D) were shopping

9. If I saw the damage to your house, I _________ you an estimate for the repair costs.
(A) could give (B) have given
(C) give (D) gave

10. Mr. Burnage may contact some successful local business owners ________ extra funding be required to start his new restaurant.
(A) when (B) should
(C) in fact (D) through

11. __________ you have any problem, please call us right away to find the solutions.
(A) Had (B) Have
(C) Should (D) Were

12. Defective merchandise may be exchanged if you ___________ the receipt within a week of your purchase.
(A) present (B) had presented
(C) will present (D) would present

13. _____________ the human resources department directly if you experience any problems.
(A) Contacting (B) Please contact
(C) Will contact (D) Can contact

14. _______ we rearrange our schedule, we can hear his presentation tomorrow.
(A) Could (B) Should
(C) Had (D) Might

15. If automobile insurance policies covered accidental damage, few people ___________ to pay the premiums.
(A) afforded (B) could afford
(C) have afforded (D) will afford

16. If the warranty had not included a return policy, I would __________ an objection with the company.

(A) be raised (B) had raised
(C) have raised (D) been raised

17. If the purchaser had attended the jewelry auction, he would _________ an artificial diamond.

(A) has bought (B) buying
(C) be bought (D) have bought

18. Please _________ to the security guard directly if you leave much earlier than expected.

(A) will report (B) report
(C) reported (D) reporting

19. It will be very helpful if you thoroughly _________ the background of the applicants.

(A) refer (B) check
(C) advertise (D) exchange

20. If the promotional displays ____________ in a more visible spot, a greater number of customers would have purchased the products.

(A) placed (B) had been placed
(C) place (D) are placed

제9강

준동사 – to 부정사

to 부정사 – to infinitive

- **형태** : to+동사원형 – to attend, to slove ...
- **의미** : to부정사 자체는 품사가 없지만 놓이는 자리에 따라 명사, 형용사, 부사의 역할

○ 형태 : to+동사원형 (편의상 to+R(root) 혹은 to+V로 표기)
○ 준동사이므로 동사 자리에 들어갈 수 없다.
○ 부정사 자체는 품사가 없지만, 놓이는 자리에 따라 품사가 정해진다 – 명사, 형용사, 부사
○ to부정사의 의미상 주어는 to 앞에 'for + 명사/목적격대명사'로 나타낸다.
The company prepared all the food and tableware **for the guests** to use.

1. 명사 역할 (~하는 것)

주어 To look over all the terms and conditions will be challenging.
목적어 The contractor agreed to redesign the whole building as we requested.
주격 보어 Our main **goal** this year is to increase our sales overseas.
(보어로 쓰일 경우는 주어가 Goal, Aim, Purpose, Objective 가 주로 온다.)
목적격 보어 The applicant's qualifications allowed her to get a job.

○ to부정사를 목적어로 취하는 3형식 동사 (S + V + O) – 소풍동사를 기억하자!

want/wish toV	hope toV	would like toV	expect toV
plan toV	aim toV	agree toV	refuse/decline toV

intend toV	strive toV	decide toV	promise toV
pledge toV	need toV	afford toV	manage toV
try toV	fail toV	tend toV	offer toV

○ to부정사를 목적격보어로 취하는 5형식 동사(행동유발 동사)

능동(V+O+O.C) →	수동(be p.p+O.C)	능동(V+O+O.C) →	수동(be p.p+O.C)
ask A toV	be asked toV	invite A toV	be instructed toV
request A toV	be request toV	require A toV	be required toV
allow A toV	be allowed toV	permit A toV	be permitted toV
encourage A toV	be encouraged toV	expect A toV	be expected toV
advise A toV	be advised toV	instruct A toV	be invited toV
force A toV	be forced toV	remind A toV	be reminded toV

2. 형용사 역할(~할, ~하려는)

ability toV	right toV	authority toV	strategy toV
attempt toV	effort toV	way toV	plan toV
time toV	decision toV	failure toV	desire toV
means/steps toV		chance/opportunity toV	

3. 부사 역할

목적 (~하기 위해서)

To encourage cooperation, the director held a meeting.

※ 목적의 의미를 강조할 때는 부정사 앞에 in order to(= so as to)를 쓴다.

원인 (~해서 / ~하게 돼서)

The CEO was pleased to announce that company would expand into Europe.

○ 형용사/분사 관용표현(be동사 + 형용사/분사 + toV)

예정	be supposed/expected/due/scheduled toV ~하기로 되어있다 be sure/certain toV 반드시 ~하다 be about toV 막 ~하려고 하다
가능	be likely/apt/liable/prone toV ~하기 쉽다, ~할 것 같다 be able/unable toV ~할 수 있다/없다 be ready toV ~할 준비가 되어있다
소망	be eager/anxious/keen toV 간절히 ~하고 싶어하다 be hesitant/reluctant/unwilling toV ~하기를 꺼리다 be willing toV 기꺼이 ~하다 be honored toV ~하게 되어 영광이다
기타	be glad/delighted/pleased toV ~하게 되어 기쁘다 be eligible/entitled toV ~할 자격이 있다 be present toV ~하기 위해 참석하다 be fortunate toV ~할 수 있어 행운이다

to 부정사 실전문제

1. _________ a capable employee, the project manager interviews many applicants during the recruitment processes.

(A) To choosing (B) For choose
(C) To choose (D) Choose

2. Some taxpayers refused ___________ the amounts of their earnings to the governments last year.

(A) reports (B) to report
(C) report (D) reported

3. The candidate wanted to _________ into the internship program at Multimedia Corporation.

(A) accept (B) be accepted
(C) have accepted (D) accepted

4. The human resources department required employees _________ ideas for improving the performance.

(A) to submit (B) submitting
(C) submitted (D) submits

5. __________ should be met to join our company which is very famous.

(A) Requiring (B) To require
(C) Requirements (D) Required

6. Cold weather is likely ________ throughout the month, with a chance of heavy rains which are expected to continue.

(A) last (B) lasted
(C) to last (D) lasting

7. __________ for the opening early doesn't mean that you become one of the company's employees.

(A) Applicants (B) Apply
(C) To apply (D) Applicable

8. Ms. Wilson will help the personnel manager ________ for the aptitude test.
(A) prepare (B) prepared
(C) prepares (D) preparation

9. Please don't forget ______________ the restaurant in order to attract more potential customers.
(A) remodeling (B) remodeled
(C) to be remodeled (D) to remodel

10. To get to the Hard Rock Cafe, _______ the elevator at the south end of the lobby.
(A) use (B) used
(C) using (D) to use

11. The restaurant will be offering customers a discount coupon ____________ its 5th anniversary.
(A) to celebrate (B) celebrates
(C) celebrated (D) in celebration

12. Employees should make an effort to ____________ in social activities after work with their colleagues.
(A) participated (B) participating
(C) participation (D) participate

13. The purpose of the program is _________ museum staff with the know-how and feedback to set priorities and identify areas for change.
(A) provide (B) provided
(C) provision (D) to provide

14. The CEO believes that the staff will be able ____________ on the Albers Project once the staff evaluations are completed.
(A) concentrate (B) concentrating
(C) to concentration (D) to concentrate

15. _________ diversify its healthcare product line, Hao Ihen, Inc., has entered into a partnership with Scheider Biotechnology.
(A) As far as (B) In order to
(C) Consequently (D) Furthermore

16. The new prototype is expected _________ the team an idea of weather the vehicle design is stable at high speeds.
(A) giving (B) give
(C) to give (D) to be given

17. The Dogwood Company is pleased ___________ that you can get 50 percent off all the newly released products.
(A) announce (B) to announce
(C) announcement (D) be announcing

18. In order _____ Mr. Holt to contact you, please leave your phone number.
(A) to (B) of
(C) for (D) with

19. Those who are looking for jobs are __________ to bring at least 10 resumes to the job fair and to be ready for short interviews.
(A) advised (B) criticized
(C) monitored (D) excused

20. The World Heritage Organization is dedicated to ___________ the natural characteristics of Dargo Islands
(A) preservation
(B) preserve
(C) preserved
(D) preserving

제10강

준동사편 – 동명사

1. to부정사와 달리 명사 역할만 한다.

주어 Complying with safety rules is necessary to maintain a safe environment.

동사의 목적어 Due to some errors, the company suggests calling the toll-free number.

전치사의 목적어 By signing this form, you agree to the revised terms and conditions.

보어 The manager's original idea was visiting the plants once a week.

※ 주어, 주격보어의 Ving는 toV로 대체 가능하다.

2. 동명사 VS 명사

○ 동사의 성질이 남아 있어 동명사는 뒤에 목적어가 올 수 있고 명사는 목적어를 취할 수 없다.

After completing this workshop, MS. Fields will be in charge of **supervising this plant**.

뒤에 of this plant가 오면 전치사구 생략가능하며 목적어가 없으므로 명사가 와야 함.

→ MS. Fields will be in charge of **supervision (of this plant)**.

○ 관사 a/an 뒤에는 동명사가 올 수 없고 앞에는 일반 명사가 올 수 없다.

There was a decrease in the registration rate for the conference this year.

The management is in the process of establishing a new set of guidelines.

○ 명사는 형용사의 수식을 받고, 동명사는 부사의 수식을 받는다.

※ –ing 형태의 일반명사

market 시장	marketing 마케팅	plan 계획	planning 계획 수립
seat 좌석	seating 좌석 배치	staff 직원	staffing 직원 채용
fund 자금	funding 자금 조달	open 열린(a.)	opening 공석
caterer 출장연회 업체		catering 출장연회 서비스	

○ 동명사를 목적어로 취하는 3형식 동사 (S + V + O)

고려, 제안	consider -ing	suggest -ing	recommend -ing
중단, 지속	finish -ing	complete -ing	keep -ing
	quit -ing	give up -ing	discontinue -ing
기타	enjoy -ing	include -ing	avoid -ing
	deny -ing	dislike -ing	mind -ing
	delay -ing	postpone -ing	

○ 동명사 관용표현

keep (on) -ing 계속 ~하다
by -ing ~함으로써
be capable of -ing ~할 수 있다
be busy (in) -ing ~하느라 바쁘다
on/upon -ing ~하자마자
be worth -ing ~할 가치가 있다
cannot help -ing ~하지 않을 수 없다
spend 시간/돈 (on/in) -ing ~에 시간/돈을 쓰다
prevent A from -ing A가 ~하는 것을 막다
have difficulty/problems/trouble (in) -ing ~하는 데 어려움을 겪다
have a hard time (in) -ing ~하는 데 어려움을 겪다

동명사 실전문제

1. ________ to the construction site must wear a protective helmet and glasses.
(A) Visit (B) Visitors
(C) Visiting (D) Visits

2. Due to certain __________, only cities with populations over 200,000 were considered for the new office.
(A) limit (B) limiting
(C) limited (D) limitations

3. Lulpite Corporation discontinued _________ home appliance.
(A) to produce (B) producing
(C) production (D) produced

4. The theater owner prevented the audience from ___________ the performance.
(A) recording (B) record
(C) to record (D) recorded

5. By _______ the assembly-line process, total production quantities can be increased.
(A) updates (B) updating
(C) updated (D) update

6. After _______ reviewing the seating chart, let me know what changes should be made.
(A) carefully (B) to care
(C) careful (D) care

7. Purchasing a movie ticket through the Web site _________ only a few minutes.
(A) taken (B) take
(C) takes (D) taking

8. A good way of ___________ customers is to give them a money-back guarantee.
(A) attracts (B) attraction
(C) attracting (D) attracted

9. Festival _________ can try authentic dishes from around the world.
(A) Attending (B) Attends
(C) Attendees (D) Attendance

10. The person in charge of dealing with urgent __________ is Mr. Morales.
(A) request (B) requesting
(C) requested (D) requests

11. We at Medosa Hotel strongly recommend __________ rooms more than six weeks in advance during the summer time.
(A) books (B) to book
(C) booking (D) be booked

12. Roxen Inc. will try to attract a lot of potential buyers by ___________ advertising its website locally.
(A) effective (B) effectively
(C) more effective (D) most effective

13. Bismark Broadcasting is ____________ to providing accurate investment information to help its investors make profits.
(A) dedicated (B) dedicating
(C) dedication (D) dedicatedly

14. The Marketing manager suggested ______ the logo to enhance the image of the company.
(A) change (B) changing
(C) to change (D) changes

15. Before _________ to buy an apartment in Charlton, Mr. Russell consulted his colleague about the area.
(A) decide (B) decision
(C) decides (D) deciding

16. _________ on technology will eventually increase productivity and make profits.
(A) Spending (B) Spent
(C) Spend (D) Spendable

17. Before the end of the year, the supervisors must spend time ______ appraisals of each worker's contribution to the company.

(A) wrote (B) write
(C) written (D) writing

18. Employees must not download programs onto their computer without __________ the network administrator first.

(A) notifies (B) notifying
(C) notified (D) notification

19. __________ shifts for employees is one of a manager's most important responsibilities.

(A) Arranges (B) Arranging
(C) Arrangement (D) Arrange

20. Please keep in mind that all outdoor activities are subject to __________ without notice.

(A) cancellation (B) canceling
(C) canceled (D) cancel

제11강

준동사편 – 분사

1. 분사의 종류

○ 현재분사 – (동사원형 + –ing) : singing, running, touching...

: 명사를 꾸밀 때 분사와 명사의 관계가 능동/진행일 때 사용. '~하는'의 의미
수식 대상이 감정을 유발시키는 사물이면 현재분사를 쓴다.

That Hyundai Motors has become the leader in the electric car industry is quite **interesting**.

○ 과거분사 – (동사원형 + –ed) : revised, reduced, attatched...

: 명사를 꾸밀 때 분사와 명사의 관계가 수동/완료일 때 사용. '~된', '~되는'의 의미
수식 대상이 감정을 느끼는 사람/회사면 과거분사를 쓴다.

Mr. Park was very **disappointed** with the sales this year.

2. 수식하는 형용사 역할

명사 앞 수식 Companies should not provide any **misleading** information.

명사 뒤 수식 Any requests **approved** by a supervisor will be processed immediately.

3. 보어로 사용되는 형용사 역할

주격 보어 The management was **thrilled** about releasing a new line of clothing.

목적격 보어 Most of our travel client found the spa tour **relaxing**.

○ 현재분사 관용표현

challenging task 힘든 과제	promising candidate 유망한 후보자
encouraging remark 격려의 말	surrounding area 주변 지역
leading supplier 선도적인 납품업체	demanding customer 까다로운 고객
leading complaint 주된 불편사항들	growing business 성장하는 사업
preceding years 지난 몇 년	lasting impression 지속적인 인상
rewarding discussion 가치 있는 토론	missing luggage 분실한 짐
contributing author 기고 작가	outstanding debts 미불 채무
existing equipment 기존 장비	outstanding painter 뛰어난 작가
inviting atmosphere 매력적인 분위기	remaining staff 남아있는 직원
misleading information 허위 정보	approaching summer 다가오는 여름
overwhelming number 압도적인 숫자	rising cost 오르는 가격

○ 과거분사 관용표현

accomplished chef 노련한 요리사	established company 자리를 잡은 회사
attached file 첨부 파일	reduced cost 감소된 비용
damaged goods 파손된 물품	reserved seat 예약된 좌석
enclosed form 첨부 양식	assigned budget 배당된 예산
experienced employee 경력 직원	customized product 주문 제작 상품
preferred method 바람직한 방식	distinguished scholar 뛰어난 학자
revised itinerary 수정된 여행 일정	limited time 제한된 시간
complicated problem 복잡한 문제	qualified applicant 적격인 지원자
dedicated employee 헌신적인 직원	skilled engineer 숙련된 기술자
detailed information 자세한 정보	written statement 서면 진술
desired result 바라던 결과	required document 필요 서류
proposed initiative 제안된 계획안	updated manual 업데이트 된 메뉴얼

4. 분사구문

: 분사는 형용사 역할을 하고, 분사구문은 부사의 역할을 한다.
보통 콤마 앞이 부사절이지만 콤마 뒤가 부사절일 수도 있다.

조건 **If you obtain a store card**, you will enjoy benefits each time you shop here.
= **Obtaining a store card**, you will enjoy benefits each time you shop here.

양보 **Although he interviewed all the applicants**, the director could not find suitable candidate.
= **Interviewing all the applicants**, the director couldn't find suitable candidate.

이유 **Because she was inspired by a local business owner**, Ms. Joo is studying to become a chef.
= **(Being) inspired by a local business owner**, Ms. Joo is studying to become a chef.

시간 **After he had talked with all the employees**, the CEO decided to implement flexible working hours.
= **Having talked with all the employees**, the CEO decided to implement flexible working hours.

※ 분사구문의 의미를 명확히 전달하기 위해 부사절 접속사를 그대로 남겨 두기도 한다.

(Before) signing the paperwork, please check your shipments for damage.

※ 동시동작(~함에 따라 / ~하면서)
: 동시에 일어나는 일을 나타낼 때 분사구문 앞에 with를 붙여 쓴다.

With the ceremony approaching, the committee is busy preparing for the occasion.

※ be p.p가 수동으로 축약될 때 being p.p가 되는 경우나 be동사가 축약되어 being이 되며 being은 생략가능하다. 이 경우에서 문장 맨 앞이나 부사절 접속사 뒤에 수동태나 전치사가 바로 올 수도 있다.

While they are in London, travelers should eat at a traditional fish-and-chip restaurant.
→ While (being) in London, travelers should eat at a traditional fish-and-chip restaurant.

5. 감정을 나타내는 분사

감정을 나타내는 현재분사는 주로 감정을 줄 수 있는 대상인 경우 – 사건, 사물
Some of the economic numbers have been **disappoingting** because they did not meet expectations

감정을 나타내는 과거분사는 주로 감정을 받는 대상인 경우 – 사람
The children became **excited** when the clowns arrived at the birthday party.

감정동사	현재분사	과거분사
excite 신나게 하다	exciting 신나는, 들뜨게 하는	excited 신이 난, 들뜬
please 기쁘게 하다	pleasing 기쁘게 하는	pleased 기뻐하는, 만족스러운
surprise 놀라게 하다	surprising 놀라운	surprised 놀란
disappoint 실망시키다	disappointing 실망시키는	disappointed 실망한
satisfy 만족시키다	satisfying 만족을 주는	satisfied 만족한
interest 흥미를 일으키다	interesting 흥미 있는	interested 흥미를 가진
confuse 혼동을 일으키다	confusing 혼동을 일으키는	confused 혼란스러워 하는
amuse 즐겁게 하다	amusing 재미있는	amused 재미있어 하는
tire 지치게 하다	tiring 피곤하게 하는	tired 피곤한, 지친
disturb 방해하다	disturbing 방해가 되는	disturbed 방해 받은, 산란한
embarrass 당황하게 하다	embarrassing 당황스럽게 하는	embarrassed 당황한, 난처한
worry 걱정시키다	worrying 걱정을 끼치는	worried 근심에 싸인

분사 실전문제

1. New workers must attend their __________ training session held in the conference room at 10 A.M.
(A) assigned (B) assigns
(C) assign (D) assigning

2. Jenny's Fight is one of the most _______ movies of the month.
(A) anticipation (B) anticipated
(C) anticipating (D) anticipate

3. The Cha clinic, ________ excellent medical service, was named the best clinic.
(A) providing (B) provides
(C) provided (D) provide

4. Buses' ________ repairs are needed in order to keep bus passengers safe.
(A) extensive (B) extend
(C) extending (D) extends

5. Newly hired employees are required to attend a very ________ three-week training course prior to starting to work.
(A) demand (B) demanded
(C) demanding (D) demands

6. By focusing on the love story of young people, the play writer made a common story ________________.
(A) excitement (B) exciting
(C) excitably (D) excited

7. If the manual is __________, please call the service center.
(A) confusing (B) confusion
(C) confuses (D) confused

8. We were ____________ because of the restaurant's poor service.
(A) disappointing (B) disappointed
(C) disappoint (D) disappoints

9. The musical production company will hold auditions for ___________ dancers next Friday on April 11.
(A) to experience (B) experience
(C) experiences (D) experienced

10. To keep employees ___________ of the most recent project developments, we update the company Web site daily.
(A) inform (B) informed
(C) informing (D) informs

11. Before assembling this product, please read entirely the instructions _________ in this box.
(A) providing (B) provided
(C) provision (D) to provide

12. The personnel manager will meet with the members of the hiring committee to deliver his opinions after ______ candidates.
(A) interview (B) interviews
(C) interviewing (D) interviewed

13. Any person who is ______ in volunteering his or her time for the campaign should send this office a letter of intent.
(A) interest (B) interested
(C) interesting (D) interestingly

14. According to the federal rules, investor __________ to buy more than 20% of a corporation's stock are required to file notice five business days in advance.
(A) intending (B) are intending
(C) intended (D) intend

15. Initially, your __________ loan application will be sent to the loan office, who must check your credit standing before making any preliminary decision.
(A) completing (B) completed
(C) completion (D) completely

16. Even though Lester Robinson has a minor role in the movie, his moving performance leaves a ________ impression on the audience.
(A) lasts (B) lasting
(C) lasted (D) lastly

17. When ________ an intersection, you should slow down and watch for traffic coming in every direction.
(A) approach (B) approaches
(C) approached (D) approaching

18. Sheridon College will allow an ___________ deadline for those students who were unable to access the school's website last week.
(A) extend (B) extends
(C) extensive (D) extended

19. ________ exceeded this year's goals for sales, all employees in Muller Publishing received a substantial bonus.
(A) Being (B) To have
(C) Having (D) To be

20. Visitors must park their cars in the _____________ area of the Upper Campus lot.
(A) designated (B) designation
(C) designating (D) designates

제12강

접속사 – 등위, 상관 접속사

1. 등위접속사

동일한 품사나 구조를 대등하게 연결한다(so, far는 절과 절만 연결함).

and 그리고	or 또는	but/yet 그러나	so 그래서	for 왜냐하면

명사&명사 We will offer you food and drink.

형용사&형용사 The Darese Spa offers a relaxing and elegant atmosphere.

동사&동사 Please e-mail me or call my secretary at extension 320.

전치사구&전치사구 Design staff are advised to put the files in a folder or on the shelf.

절&절 Mr. Kwon is unable to attend the meeting, so Ms. shin will attend in his place.

2. 상관 접속사

both A and B　A와 B 둘 다 either A or B　A와 B 둘 중 하나 neither A nor B　A와 B 둘 다 아닌 not only A but (also) B = B as well as A A뿐 아니라 B도	between A and B　A와 B 사이에 whether A or B　A이거나 혹은 B이거나 A rather than B　B라기보다는 A not A but B = B but not A A가 아니라 B

Both Sue and Kate are my coworkers.

James is not only talented but also hardworking.

※ 수 일치 : A and B는 복수동사, either A or B / neither A nor B는 B에 일치시킨다.

Neither they nor she thinks that she will be promoted.

제13강

접속사 – 부사절의 접속사

1. 부사절 접속사 – 각 접속사의 뜻을 정확히 알고 문장을 해석해서 찾아야한다!

접속사 + 주어 + 동사, 주어 + 동사
(부사절)

If you have an questions, feel free to contact us.
Now that the tunnerls have been completed, the driving time has been cut in half.
Even though the budget was not sufficient, the project was successfully completed.

시간	when / as / by the time ~할 때 as soon as ~하자마자 while ~하는 동안	before ~ 전에 since ~ 이래로 until ~할 때까지	after ~ 후에
이유	because/as/since ~ 때문에	now that ~이므로/~니까	in that ~라는 점에서
양보	although / though / even though / even if 비록 ~일지라도 while/whereas ~인 반면, ~이지만		
조건	if / provided (that) / providing (that) 만약 ~라면 on condition (that) ~라는 조건으로, 만약 ~라면 assuming (that) / supposing (that) ~라고 가정하면 unless / if ~ not 만약 ~이 아니라면		once 일단 ~하면 in case ~하는 경우에는 only if ~하기만 하면 as long as / as far as ~하는 한
목적	so (that) + 주어 + can/may 주어가 ~할 수 있도록 in order that + 주어 + can/may 주어가 ~하기 위하여		
결과	so + 형용사/부사 + that … 매우 ~해서 …하다 such + a(n) + A(형용사) + B(명사) + that 매우 A한 B라서 ~하다		

기타	as if / as though 마치 ~인 것처럼 whether ~ or / or not ~이든 아니든, ~와 상관없이 except that ~라는 것을 제외하고 considering (that) / given (that) ~을 고려할 때

○ **부사절 접속사 VS 전치사**

- 접속사와 의미는 같다. 하지만, 접속사 뒤에는 **문장**이, 전치사 뒤에는 **명사**가 붙는다.

	접속사 + 문장 / 축약형태	전치사 + 명사(구)
시간	when / as / by the time while until as soon as before after	at/on/in during/for by/until (up)on-ing before / prior to after/following
이유	because/as/since	because of / due to / owing to / on account of
양보	although / though / even though / even if	despite / in spite of / notwithstanding
조건/경우	unless / if not in case / if	without / but for in case of / in the event of
목적	so that / in order that	for the purpose of
대조/기타	while/whereas given that	compared with given

While **a new electrical system is being installed**, the factory will be closed.
접속사 + 문장

→ During **the installation of a new electrical system**, the factory will be closed.
전치사 + 명사

○ 관계부사 - 의미가 비슷하지만 Part5 에서는 대부분 오답으로 등장한다.

양보	~임에도 불구하고	however, nevertheless, nonetheless
결과	따라서, 결과적으로	hence, therefore, thus, as a result
부가	더욱이, 게다가	besides, furthermore, moreover, above all, in addition
추가	사실상, 정말로	indeed, in fact
대조	반대로, 이에 반해	contrarily, in contrast, on the other hand, on the contrary
순서	그후에, 다음에	then, thereafter, afterwards
가정	그렇지않으면	otherwise
전환	그동안, 한편	meanwhile

등위접속사, 부사절접속사 실전문제

1. Jeju-do is a popular tourist location, _____ you can enjoy the magnificent scenery.
   (A) despite (B) due to
   (C) and (D) although

2. _______ the free delivery service, the company offers customers a discount coupon.
   (A) Furthermore (B) Due to
   (C) Yet (D) In addition to

3. The store is ______ small that it provides no seating.
   (A) so (B) very
   (C) truly (D) such

4. _________ people agreed the merger's terms at the meeting, they still must gain formal approval.
   (A) In spite of (B) So as to
   (C) Regarding (D) Even though

5. The Internet can be used in the underground parking lot ________ in stores and offices.
   (A) as well as (B) both
   (C) either (D) not only

6. People modified safety regulations last week _________ follow new standards.
   (A) when (B) in order to
   (C) due to (D) in addition

7. We will not offer anyone our customers' information ________ their consent.
   (A) although (B) unless
   (C) when (D) without

8. ________ RA company has done so well, the company will be opening anoter branch in Daejeon.
   (A) Unless (B) Since
   (C) Therefore (D) Rather

9. The line of the suitcase is _________ fashionable and durable.
(A) both (B) either
(C) neither (D) as well as

10. ________ the increase in fuel prices, the United Airline will probably increase the air fare.
(A) Provided (B) Given
(C) Regardless (D) When

11. ___________ their previous model was quite popular among teens, few expect the next one to be as attractive.
(A) In spite of (B) Even
(C) Regardless (D) But

12. Greenychi Safety Shipping assures you that all shipments will be delivered on time _______ remote their destinations might be.
(A) no matter how (B) insofar as
(C) nevertheless (D) in order that

13. Lexington Museum is seeking a new curator not only to organize new exhibits _____ to give tours on special occasions.
(A) but also (B) only if
(C) or (D) and

14. Client requests for DNA tests cannot proceed ________ a deposit of $100 is received.
(A) despite (B) even
(C) until (D) prior to

15. ________ Novana Industry's overall revenue has decreased for the last two years, some departments have seen slight increases in sales.
(A) While (B) Since
(C) Instead (D) However

16. The former CEO, Kate Hatfield, had no choice but to resign when _______ with stiff resistance from both inside and outside the company.
(A) face (B) faced
(C) facing (D) faces

17. ________ the January company newsletter is published, the final decision on the outsourcing contract will have been made.

(A) By the time (B) In order to
(C) Following (D) Now that

18. Over 2,000 people attended last Sunday's International Food Fair, ________ the heavy rains that swamped parts of the area.

(A) while (B) whereas
(C) notwithstanding (D) moreover

19. ________ more people are connected through social media, it has become much easier for consumers to share product reviews.

(A) Instead of (B) Now that
(C) Because of (D) As if

20. ________ the budget allocated for this project is strictly limited, it is important to consider cost-efficiency at each phase of the project.

(A) Even if (B) Because of
(C) Unless (D) Given

제14강

접속사 – 명사절의 접속사

1. 명사절 접속사 : 문장을 명사로 활용하는 것!

- 접속사는 단순히 연결요소가 아닌, 문장을 하나의 품사 역할로 만들어 주는 역할을 한다는 것이 중요한 포인트!

주어 **That all new employees will attend the seminar** is known to management.
타동사의 목적어 Every staff wondered **whether/if we should find a new supplier or not.**
보어 The fact is **that the team needs additional time to complete the task.**

※ 명사절 접속사는 자체가 명사역할을 하므로 선행사가 없다.
보어자리에 절이 올 때는 명사절만 쓴다(형용사절 X).
목적어 자리에 나오는 명사절 접속사 that은 생략할 수 있다.
that 절은 콤마, 전치사 뒤에 올 수 없다(부사절 접속사 in that 제외).
that절, whether절은 주어, 목적어, 보어로 쓸 수 있지만 if절은 목적어로만 쓴다.

○ **명사절을 이끄는 that** : 완전한 문장의 형태가 오며 주어, 목적어, 보어의 역할을 한다.

That the CEO approved the plan was surprising.
The management announced **that the CEO approved the plan**.

○ **명사절을 이끄는 what** : 불완전한 문장의 형태가 오며 주어, 목적어, 보어의 역할을 한다.

What he writes becomes a bestseller.
The writer wanted to share **what he experienced from his travels.**

that	주어, 목적어, 보어 역할	완전한 문장이 온다
what	주어, 목적어, 보어 역할	불완전한 문장이 온다. (주어나 목적어가 빠짐)

○ 형용사 + that절

be aware that ~을 알다	be happy that ~해서 기쁘다
be conviced that ~을 확신하다	be glad that ~해서 기쁘다
be confident that ~을 확신하다	be delighted that ~해서 기쁘다
be afraid that ~을 두려워하다	make sure that ~을 확실히 하다
	be sure that ~을 확실히 하다

○ that절을 목적어로 취하는 동사

announce (that) ~을 발표하다	recommend (that) ~을 추천하다
indicate (that) ~을 나타내다	suggest (that) ~을 제안하다
mention (that) ~라고 언급하다	propose (that) ~을 제안하다
explain (that) ~을 설명하다	ask (that) ~을 요청하다
note (that) ~라고 언급하다, 유념하다	ensure (that) 확실히 ~ 하다
determine (that) ~을 결정하다	make sure (that) 확실히 ~ 하다

○ whether (or not) + 완전한 문장 / whether + 완전한 문장 + (or not)

: ~할지 말지, ~인지 아닌지

Whether (or not) we will assign overtime to meet the deadline still hasn't been decide.

We are still not sure whether the operations team will move to our office (or not).

※ 명사절 접속사 whether에서는 or, or not을 생략할 수 있다.

○ 의문대명사 who(m)/which/what + 불완전한 문장

○ 의문형용사 whose/which/what + 명사 + 불완전한 문장

Mr. Kim knows whose desk the new intern will use.

Please let me know which sample should be returned.

※ which가 의문형용사 일 때는 사람도 꾸밈

○ 의문부사 when/where/why/how + 완전한 문장

○ 의문사들의 축약

: toV 뒤에 목적어 있으면 완전(whether/의문부사) 없으면 불완전(의문대명사/의문형용사)

We haven't determined whether we should close the main entrance.

→ We haven't determined whether to close the main entrance.

○ 접속사 문제 해결하는 순서

1. 접속사 덩어리를 파악하자
2. 덩어리의 역할을 명사, 형용사, 부사 중 어느 것으로 쓰였지를 파악한다.
3. 보기에서 해당하는 접속사를 선택한다.
4. 각 접속사의 특징을 파악하고 정답을 고른다.

명사절의 접속사 실전문제

1. Flight attendants can guarantee ________ United Airline's customers stay comfortable during the flight.
   (A) that (B) if
   (C) whether (D) because

2. ________ the product is opened or not, you can get a full refund for defective products.
   (A) That (B) Whether
   (C) Either (D) What

3. The instruction manual states _______ the food processor can be used for vegetables and grains.
   (A) but (B) that
   (C) so (D) while

4. The president will decide ______ to merge with the company.
   (A) whether (B) either
   (C) even if (D) so that

5. City officials insist ______ new parking meters will not increase parking costs.
   (A) that (B) what
   (C) if (D) whether

6. The company will delay this week's newsletter ______ employees should still learn how to use the new publishing software.
   (A) whether (B) because
   (C) in addition (D) therefore

7. Please be aware _______ the dress code policy can be changed.
   (A) that (B) whether
   (C) if (D) because

8. The objective of these team meetings is to review and assess how __________ our advertising companies are performing.
(A) effect (B) effects
(C) effectively (D) effectiveness

9. Advocates of working at home often talk about ________ well it suits those who decide to work part-time.
(A) how (B) therefore
(C) only (D) most

10. Our supervisor wants to know ______ the final revision will be made to the contract.
(A) on (B) as to
(C) what (D) when

11. We started the project _______ will change an old warehouse into a wonderful restaurant.
(A) that (B) nor
(C) unless (D) yet

12. _____ RED company builds a new factory in Seoul depends on the approval from the Mayor of Seoul.
(A) While (B) Whether
(C) Although (D) Despite

13. Ms. Hwang must decide _______ to submit the proposal to the city council by the end of the week.
(A) whether (B) whereas
(C) if (D) unless

14. The Fabolia Dance School will hold an information session on April 7 for _______ interested in signing up for summer classes.
(A) whoever (B) they
(C) anyone (D) them

15. _____ needs an income verification form should ask Ms. Roh in the Accounting Department.
(A) Some (B) Who
(C) Whoever (D) Anyone

16. ______ the year-end profit shares will be half of last year's is disappointing news to the entire staff.

(A) What (B) Although
(C) That (D) Because

17. At the press conference, the spokesperson of Kelton Incorporated stated ______ the company has planned for the next year.

(A) what (B) how
(C) when (D) that

18. _____ Mr. Greene has been promoted twice in three years is proof of his outstanding ability in the field of marketing.

(A) That (B) But
(C) Since (D) After

19. JST Jewelry customers can get 10 percent off their purchase _____ they spend $30 or more.

(A) than (B) that
(C) even (D) as long as

20. Due to the availability of online video streaming services, it is not common for people nowadays to just watch _______ appears on television.

(A) anyone (B) whatever
(C) unless (D) however

제15강

접속사편 – 형용사절의 접속사

1. 관계대명사절 – 문장이 명사를 수식하는 형용사의 역할을 한다.

: 접속사 + 주어/소유격/목적어 → 관계대명사

We use the building materials and they are the highest quality ones available.

→ We use the building materials which are the highest quality ones available.

선행사	주격	소유격	목적격
사람	who	whose	who(m)
사물, 동물	which	whose / of which	which
사람, 사물, 동물	that	-	that

※ 선행사 뒤에 ,가 오는 경우 that은 쓸 수 없고 who/which만 쓴다.
관사와 소유격 같이 쓰지 않는다.

○ 목적격 관계대명사는 생략할 수 있다.

The server (whom) they remember answered all their questions about the menu choice.

○ 주격 관계대명사 + be 동사는 생략할 수 있다.

The man (who is) working on the budget report is Mr. Yao.

○ 전치사 + 목적격 관계대명사(whom/which)

There was a board meeting during which the directors talked about the expansion plan.

Confidential e-mails should be read only by the person to whom they are addressed.

○ 수량표현(one, some, many, none, several...) + of + 목적격 관계대명사(whom/which)

The interns, some of whom are local college students, learned their duties quickly.

The new staff lounge, half of which has not been painted, is still under construction.

ex) The entire staff of Harvard University consists of around 12,000 people, many of _________ are employed by the Department of Medicine.

(A) which (B) whose

(C) whom (D) those

※ 전치사 + 목적격 관계대명사에서는 whom을 who로 쓸 수 없다.

2. 관계부사 – 관계대명사와 차이점은 선행사가 시간, 장소, 원인, 방법이며 뒷문장이 완전

: 접속사 + 부사 → 관계부사

	선행사	관계부사	전치사 + 관계대명사
시간	time, day, year 등	when	in/on/at/during which
장소	place, site, factory 등	where	in/on/at which
이유	the reason	why	for which

This is the room, we hold a meeting in the room.

→ This is the room, we hold a meeting in which.

→ This is the room where we hold a meeting.

○ 관계대명사 VS 관계부사 : 뒤에 불완전한 절이 오면 관계대명사(소유격 제외), 완전한 절이 오면 관계부사를 선택한다. 부사를 생략했기 때문에 관계부사는 완전한 절을 이끈다.

3. 동격의 that(형용사절 역할)

: 명사 + that 뒤에 완전한 절이 온다. 명사와 절의 등호 역할

the fact that ~라는 사실	the idea that ~라는 발상
the news that ~라는 소식	the report that ~라는 보고
the rumor that ~라는 소문	the conclusion that ~라는 결론
the evidence that ~라는 증거	the statement that ~라는 진술
the opinion that ~라는 의견	the assurance that ~라는 확신

4. 복합 관계대명사(부사절/명사절 역할)

whoever 누가 ~하든 (부사절), ~하는 사람은 누구든 (명사절, = anyone who)
whomever 누가 ~하든(부사절), ~하는 사람은 누구든 (명사절, = anyone whom)
whichever 어떤 것을 ~하든 (부사절), ~하는 것은 어떤 것이든 (명사절, = anything that)
whatever 무엇을 ~하든 (부사절), ~하는 것은 무엇이든 (명사절, = anything that)

※ 복합관계대명사는 '선행사 + 관계대명사'로 선행사가 필요 없다.

5. 복합 관계부사(부사절 역할)

whenever 언제 ~하든(= at any time when), 언제 ~하더라도(= no matter when)
wherever 어디에 ~하든(= at any place where), 어디서 ~하더라도(= no matter where)
however 어떻게 ~하든(= by whatever means), 아무리 ~하더라도(= no matter how)

형용사절의 접속사 실전문제

1. Many of the applicants _______ applied for the marketing department were highly qualified.
(A) they (B) when
(C) who (D) what

2. The proposal ______ we rejected will be reviewed by the board of directors.
(A) which (B) whom
(C) who (D) whose

3. Most customers want the products made by Star company, _______ advertisement appears in print and on TV.
(A) why (B) whose
(C) which (D) that

4. The manual which __________ the dress code policy will be on the desk.
(A) describe (B) describing
(C) describes (D) to describe

5. The products that are ________ by the Angel firm are good and durable.
(A) produce (B) produced
(C) producing (D) production

6. __________ who are not offered their magazines by 2:00 P.M. should contact the customer service center.
(A) Subscribers (B) Subscriber
(C) Subscription (D) Subscriptions

7. Mrs. Kim requested that ______ has a nutritious meal.
(A) she (B) her
(C) hers (D) herself

8. Red Cedar elementary school, ________ served as Victoria's first school, has been named a top school.
(A) while (B) which
(C) where (D) that

9. One of the employees you hired _____ often absent from work.
(A) is (B) are
(C) be (D) to be

10. A training session for those ______ have just joined our company will be held in the conference room.
(A) who (B) which
(C) they (D) whom

11. Some record players that _________ to SS Warehouses were defective.
(A) shipped (B) was shipped
(C) were shipped (D) shipping

12. A list of employees _____ are promoted to the manager will be posted on the board tomorrow.
(A) who (B) which
(C) what (D) whom

13. All articles in this week's newsletter were written by undergraduate students _________ want to be a professional writer.
(A) because (B) who
(C) whose (D) what

14. Groove Construction won this year's Building Award for its environmentally-friendly project that ___________ by Ms. Schmidt.
(A) is overseeing (B) has overseen
(C) was overseen (D) overseen

15. The PR manager could not start the presentation because the reference material ________ requested was not ready.
(A) she (B) that
(C) was (D) whose

16. Thomas Wyatt's sculptures are purchased by customers _______ tastes in art are sophisticated.
(A) who
(B) each
(C) whose
(D) what

17. To visit the headquarters of Harington Corporation, please take Highway 11 south to Exit 3, _______ is next to the Eliot Building.
(A) which
(B) where
(C) that
(D) who

18. The Center One Building, _____ which DGN Industries has resided since it was founded, needs a lot of updating and repair.
(A) in
(B) from
(C) until
(D) down

19. Many customers participated in the product survey conducted by Hrudy Furniture, ________ advertisements appear in magazines and newspapers.
(A) whose
(B) its
(C) which
(D) what

20. Miles Shipping first began using larger trucks for prompt delivery, all of _____ were imprinted with the company's unique logo.
(A) them
(B) it
(C) whom
(D) which

제16강

토익 독해

Questions 1-2 refer to the following e-mail.

To: Jinsoo Park
From: Hemo Customer Service
Subject: Access Denied
Date: June 1

Our records show that you have attempted to log in to your online account five times with an incorrect password. As a result, your account cannot be accessed. Please do not create a new user account, as this may cause problems with paying your bill online. In order to set a new password and restore your account, click on the link below.

http://www.hemo.com/passwordrequest12

For safety reasons, you will have to correctly answer questions about recent deposits and withdrawals. After this, your account will be completely recovered.

If you require additional assistance, please call at 031-555-5584.

Hemo Customer Service

1. What is suggested about Mr.Park?
   (A) He accessed a Web site from a mobile device.
   (B) He forgot his password
   (C) He added his spouse as an account holder.
   (D) He made more than one account.

2. What type of company is Hemo?

(A) A Web site developer
(B) An Internet service provider
(C) An online shopping mall
(D) A financial institution

어휘

access: v. 접근하다 n. 접근
deny: v. 부인하다
attempt: v. 시도하다
account: n. 계좌
restore: v. 복구하다
deposit: n. 예금, 예치
withdrawal: n. 인출
completely: adv. 완전히

Questions 1-2 refer to the following letter.

Dear Ms. Umaga:

We are pleased that you have chosen Explorer Voyage Travel Service to help you plan your upcoming trip to Greece. We have received your registration form and deposit. You will soon be receiving an invoice listing your payments and the balance due.
Please make sure that we receive your final payment by December 30 to avoid any late fees. Also, if you decided to cancel your trip, you must notify us in writing at least 10 days before your departure date to receive a refund.

Enclosed is a copy of "Are you ready to Travel?" This brochure will provide you with information you may find useful in preparing for your trip, including tips about packing, shopping, and sightseeing. You may also check out our Web site for additional material.
Just log in using your account ID.

Sincerely,

Richard Donaldson
Client Services

1. What is indicated in the letter?

(A) Ms. Umaga needs to correct her registration form.
(B) Ms. Umaga wants to delay her trip.

(C) Ms. Umaga will receive her commercial invoice.
(D) Ms. Umaga canceled her trip.

2. What was sent with the letter?
(A) An invoice
(B) A brochure
(C) A coupon
(D) A registration form

어휘

voyage 항해
upcoming 다가오는
registration 등록
deposit 예약금
invoice 송장
payment 지불
balance due 차감 부족액
avoid 피하다
late fee 연체료
cancel 취소하다
notify 알리다
in writing 서면으로
at least 최소한
departure 출발
refund 환불
enclosed 동봉된
copy 부, 권
brochure 브로셔
additional 추가적인
material 자료

Questions 1–2 refer to the following e-mail.

To: New employees
From: Myungjun Moon
Subject: April 1 workshop
Date: April 2

Welcome to Lansing Corporation. I appreciate you for participating in yesterday's workshop. I hope you found the session helpful.

My team and I are constantly trying to make our training program more informative and useful. We strive to make each session better than the last. Therefore, we want to know whether we are meeting the objectives and want attendees' feedback about the program.

We kindly ask you to go to our Web site, www.lansingcorp.com, and fill out a survey about yesterday's session.

Thank you in advance for your cooperation.

Regards,

Myungjun Moon
Coordinator, Employee Professional Development

1. Why was the e-mail written?
   (A) To congratulate some workers
   (B) To request some input
   (C) To announce an upcoming workshop
   (D) To describe a program's benefits

2. What is indicated about Mr. Moon?
   (A) She made changes to a company policy.
   (B) She regularly holds workshops.
   (C) She maintains the company Web site.
   (D) She oversees training programs.

어휘

어휘

participate: 참가하다
helpful: 도움이 되는
strive: 노력하다. 애쓰다
informative: 유익한
useful: 유용한, 도움이 되는
meet: 충족시키다
objective: 목적, 목표
attendee: 참석자
kindly: 친절하게, 정중히
fill out: 가입하다
in advance: 미리
cooperation: 협조, 협력
coordinator: 조정자, 조직자, (의견 등을) 종합하는 사람

Questions 1–3 refer to the following letter.

Dear Mr. Gonzalez

Thank you for your application for the junior accounting position here at Caxia Direct. All application and resumes are first reviewed by two of our senior staff members. If you are selected for an interview following that review, you will be contacted by our personnel officer, Ricardo Martinez, who will set up an appointment. At that time, we will ask for names and contact information for three references.

Attached is a copy of our most recent annual report, as you requested. Thank you again for your interest in Caxia Direct Corporation.

Yours truly,
Estela

1. What is the purpose of the e-mail?
   (A) To report on an interview
   (B) To request delivery of a document
   (C) To confirm receipt of an application
   (D) To inquire about an open position

2. Who will contact Mr.Gonzalez to make an appointment?
   (A) The senior accountant (B) The reocrd officer
   (C) The HR officer (D) The office manager

3. What is being sent with e-mail?
   (A) A bank statement (B) A company report
   (C) A job description (D) A staff directory

어휘

tow truck: 견인차
auto (repair) shop: 자동차 정비소
make it to: ~에 이르다, 도착하다
on time: 제시간에
fill in: 채우다, 기입하다

Questions 1–2 refer to the following information.

Product of the Month: Jenny's Coconut Soap

Jenny's Coconut Soap is handmade by LA resident Jenny Kang. Ms. Kang sells the soap locally after contracting with BY Grocery. As long as you store the soap in a cool and dry location, you can use the organic coconut oil hand soap for over three months. Other organic soaps can be used for just one month. The soap is a popular item with many BY customers and is currently on sale for $10 for a pack of three bars. It has the following benefits.

▶ Make hands soft
▶ Features a delicate scent
▶ Made of purely organic materials
▶ Have no artificial chemicals
▶ Clean hands thotoughly

Also, you can receive 10 percent off your purchase of Jenny's Coconut Soap. Simply mention discount code GD88 to a cashier at BY Grocery in LA.

1. What is the purpose of the information?
   (A) To announce the opening of a new store
   (B) To describe a cleaning procedure
   (C) To show how soap is made
   (D) To market a local resident's merchandise

2. What is mentioned about the soap?
   (A) It consists of natural ingredients.
   (B) It is sold at several locations.
   (C) It can be purchased in only single-bar packs.
   (D) It will be sold only online.

어휘

product: 제품
locally: 지역에서, 현지에서
grocery: 식료품점
organic: 유기농의
feature: 특징으로 삼다. 특징
scent: 향기
artificial: 인공적인
soap: 비누
contract: 계약하다, 계약
store: 저장하다, 보관하다
benefit: 혜택, 장점, 이득
delicate: (색깔, 향, 냄새 등이) 은은한
purely: 순전히, 오직
thoroughly: 철저히

Questions 1–2 refer to the following notice.

Office Suite Available

A 1,000-foot office suite will be available to rent on Addison Road in Beltsville starting on May 1. The ideal tenant would be a small business looking for an open floor plan. If that sounds like what you are looking for, you and your employees will be very satisfied. The space is located on the 16th floor and has windows on three sides that overlook downtown Beltsville. The view is simply amazing. The office is located in a modern building that features underground parking, three spacious elevators, and excellent security. For more information, please contact Britt Grouby at b.grouby@directrealtors.com

1. What is the purpose of the notice?
   (A) To ask for security fees
   (B) To promote a new business
   (C) To advertise an available position
   (D) To announce a space for rent

2. What is NOT stated about the suite in the notice?
   (A) It is currently unavailable.
   (B) It features multiple elevators.
   (C) It has windows on several sides.
   (D) It is on the ground floor.

어휘

rent: 임차하다
ideal: 이상적인
tenant: 세입자, 임차인
open: 탁 트인, 개방된
floor plan: 평면도
overlook: 내려다보다, 바라보다
simply: 그야말로, 정말로
amazing: 놀라운
modern: 현대적인
feature: ~이 특징이다
underground parking: 지하 주차장
spacious: 널찍한
security: 보안, 경비
ask for: ~에 대해 묻다
fee: 수수료
promote: 홍보하다
multiple: 다수의, 많은
ground floor: 1층

Questions 1~2 refer to the following advertisement.

Superior Destination SM

Very good prices for each destination

Destination	**Price**
Seoul	$199
Daejeon	$299
Daegu	$299
Busan	$310
Jeju Island	$399

Make a reservation for your discounted trip. Our Web site is www.superiorism.com. Also, browse our list of hotels so that you can find the best place to stay in the location you choose.

Terms & Conditions: Airfares are per person for economy flights. Transport to the airport via shuttle bus is included in deals, and you can have a buffet breakfast free of charge as long as you make a reservation for a hotel through our Web site.

1. What most likely is Superior Destination SM?
   (A) An airline company
   (B) A shuttle bus service
   (C) A travel agency
   (D) A hotel chain

2. What is included in deals?
   (A) Travel guidebooks
   (B) Hotel accommodations
   (C) A tour guide
   (D) A ride to the airport

어휘

superior: 우수한
destination: 목적지, 도착지
browse: (정보를 찾아) 인터넷을 돌아다니다
airfare: 항공 요금
per: ~당
transport: 운송, 수송, 이동
via: ~을 통하여, ~을 경유하여
deal: 거래
free of charge: 무료로

독해 실전문제

Test 1 이메일

From: Preeti Patel ppatel@desantech.com
To: All employees
Date: October 9
Subject: Painting

I am writing to remind everyone that the lobby will be painted tomorrow, Tuesday, October 10. The work is scheduled to begin at 8 A.M., and it should be finished by 4 P.M. All employees should avoid the lobby while the painters are working. You will need to enter and exit the building through the rear door (from the parking area) and use the staircase located to the right of that doorway.

Thank you for your cooperation. If you have any question, please contact me at extension 431.

Preeti Patel
Facilities Manager

1. What is the purpose of the e-mail?
(A) To distribute new work schedules
(B) To describe a computer program
(C) To send out a project proposal
(D) To repeat important information

2. What are employees asked to do?
(A) Complete a survey
(B) Park in a new location
(C) Use a different entrance
(D) Arrive before 8 A.M.

어휘 및 해석

Test 2 편지

Dear Huygens,

I am writing to express our gratitude to you for being a faithful customer of Genex Hair Design (GHD) for the last ten years. We greatly appreciate the fact that over the years you have helped our business grow by introducing us to your relatives and friends.

As a token of our appreciation, please accept the enclosed $20 gift certificate. It is valid for two months from the day of issue and redeemable at any our salons. Use it toward your next hair treatment or the purchase your favorite hair products.

We appreciate your business and we are looking forward to serving for many more years to come.

Your sincerely,

Marina Prasad
GHD Customer Relations Manager

1. Why was the letter written?
   (A) To announce the opening of a store
   (B) To ask for payment
   (C) To complain about a service
   (D) To thank a customer

2. What is indicated about Ms. Huygens?
   (A) She recently paid $30 for a hair treatment at GHD.
   (B) She has been working at GHD for ten years.
   (C) She has referred friends and family members to GHD.
   (D) She recently bought GHD hair products.

어휘 및 해석

Test 3 편지

Swann's department stores

Dear Frequent Customer,

Our summer sale is about to start, and we want to tell you about the substantial savings we are offering during this annual event. For two weeks only, every item in our women's clothing and accessory department will be offered to loyal customers at a marked-down price of 25 percent off the lowest price! You can view our items on our Web site at www.swannsdepartments.com

This is incredible sale will begin on June 1 and on June 14. Just bring this letter in to the store to receive our unbelievable savings. We know you won't want to miss this one!

Sincerely,

Harold Swann, Manager
Swann's Department Stores

1. What is the purpose of this letter?
   (A) To advertise a store opening
   (B) To promote a new line of clothing
   (C) To announce a change in store management
   (D) To inform readers of special savings

2. What does the letter say is available on the store's Web site?
   (A) Discount coupons
   (B) Pictures of products
   (C) Directions to the store
   (D) Store hours

어휘 및 해석

Test 4 이메일

From: customerservice@bakergifts.com

To: Harriet Goldsmith hgoldsmith@acvweb.net

Subject: Promotion

Date: January 10

Dear Ms. Goldsmith

Thank you for your recent purchase from Baker Gifts.

To show our appreciation, we'd like to offer you 15 percent off the price of your next online purchase. This promotional discount can be used on any the hundreds of products available from our Web store at www.bakergifts.com.
This offer expires on April 15. When you check out, simply center promotional code XYH9674, and 15 percent will be taken off your merchandise total.

Baker Gifts is proud of our exquisite products and exceptional customer service. We are confident you will find the perfect gift for a special person, or something well deserved for yourself.

The customer Service Team

1. What is the purpose of the e-mail?
(A) To provide information about shipping (B) To offer a discount on a future purchase
(C) To inform Ms. Goldsmith that she has won a prize (D) To explain how to buy a gift certificate

2. What is indicated about Ms. Goldsmith?
(A) She has recently bought something online. (B) She intends to purchase a gift for herself.
(C) She is a longtime customer of Baker Gifts. (D) She prefers to shop online

어휘 및 해석

Test 5 이메일

To: Robert Manilo <rmanilo@manilomasonry. com>
From: Hannah Schubert <hschubert@wlink.net>
Date: August 25
Subject: Your request

Hello Mr. Manilo,

Thank you for your e-mail. Of course I would be happy to write a comment about the job your company completed at my house. I will also post the comment in the "What Customers Are Saying" section of your company's web site, if that is OK with you.

Here is my comment:
"We are so happy we chose Manilo Masonry to install a flagstone patio, a walkway, and an outdoor fireplace at our home. The quality of the craftsmanship is top-notch, and the job was completed three days earlier than the estimated finish date. Mr. Manilo himself was present for *every* aspect of the project, from the planning stages to final inspection.
I intend to use Manila Masonry again in the future to repave our driveway."

Thanks again for doing such a great job.

Hannah Schubert

1. What did Mr. Manila ask Ms. Schubert to do?
   (A) Fill out a form
   (B) Call a prospective customer
   (C) Create a Web site for his company
   (D) Provide feedback on his work

2. What does Ms. Schubert indicate about Manila Masonry?
   (A) Its prices are reasonable
   (B) It uses the finest materials
   (C) It promises to finish jibs quickly
   (D) Its owner was personally involved in the project

3. What will Ms. Schubert probably hire Manila Masonry to work in next?
   (A) Her driveway
   (B) Her fireplace
   (C) Her patio
   (D) Her walkway

어휘 및 해석

Test 6 편지

Dear Ms. Umaga:

We are pleased that you have chosen Explorer Voyage Travel Service to help you plan your upcoming trip to Greece. We have received your registration form and deposit. You will soon be receiving an invoice listing your payments and the balance due.
Please make sure that we receive your final payment by December 30 to avoid any late fees. Also, if you decided to cancel your trip, you must notify us in writing at least 10 days before your departure date to receive a refund.

Enclosed is a copy of "Are You Ready to Travel?" This brochure will provide you with information you may find useful in preparing for your trip, including tips about packing, shopping, and sightseeing. You may also check out our Web site for additional material.
Just log in using your account ID.

Sincerely,

Richard Donaldson
Client Services

1. What is indicated in the letter?
   (A) Ms. Umaga canceled her trip.
   (B) Ms. Umaga has changed her trip itinerary.
   (C) Ms. Umaga needs to correct her registration form.
   (D) Ms. Umaga has paid part of the cost of her trip.

2. What was sent with the letter?
   (A) An invoice
   (B) A brochure
   (C) A coupon
   (D) A registration form

어휘 및 해석

Test 7 이메일

From: National Parks Visitors Bureau
To: ECSmith@eastcoast.net
Subject: Correction to Newsletter
Date: Aug 5, 5:44 am

A correction has been made to the August issue of our National Parks Newsletter. The North Mountain Views Rails to Trails package- combining two nights at the High Point Lodge, a half-day guided tour, one night at the Trail' End Inn, and two tickets on the Scenic shores Railroad- was listed incorrectly in the newsletter at $295. The actual price per person for this package is $529 plus tax and is based on double occupancy.

In addition, please note that Lake Zephyr Sports and Culture offer is valid only at the Hidden Cove Resort Hotel. Prices are for two adults, and the package includes breakfast and dinner for three days. Each additional adult with pay $222; for an additional child, the extra cost is $202. We apologize for any inconvenience.

The National Parks Visitors Bureau

1. What error was included in the August newsletter?
   (A) Trip dates were inaccurate
   (B) A tourist area was incorrectly described
   (C) A quoted price was wrong
   (D) The name of a hotel was misspelled

2. What limit is placed on the Lake Zephyr offer?
   (A) It is available only in August
   (B) It applies to only one hotel
   (C) Children are not allowed on the trip
   (D) Meals are not included in the price

어휘 및 해석

Test 8 이메일

To: Abraham Thompson Abraham@allnewphotos.com
From: Pedro Cantona pedrocan@bestcommunications.com
Sent: June 25
Re: Family Portrait

Hello, Mr. Thompson,

In celebration of their 301h wedding anniversary on July 7, I would like to give my parents a family photo. I was wondering if we could visit your studio on 22nd street in Dashvill and have the family picture taken around 6 P.M. please e-mail me to let me know if this schedule would work for you.

Several friends of mine have taken pictures in your studios in Anaheim Valley and West Wing. They recommended you, stating that pictures and the service were excellent. I really look forward to your photo shot. Hope to hear from you soon.

Pedro

1. What does the e-mail suggest about Mr. Thompson?
   (A) He has been in business for 30 years.
   (B) He has met with Mr. Cantona previously.
   (C) He lives in Dashvill.
   (D) He has studios in different locations.

2. What is Mr. Thompson asked to do?
   (A) To arrange a meeting
   (B) To provide price information
   (C) To contact Mr. Cantona
   (D) To send a photo sample

어휘 및 해석

Test 9 편지

Dear Jean,

I wanted to write you a note to thank you. I am sorry that you felt disappointed that your work responsibilities were not what you expected. I have enjoyed having your assistance with my projects.

Although the tasks we handled were not as varied as you would have liked, just think about what you and I have accomplished since September. We organized the annual small business conference, updated the association' Web site, and answered scores of inquiries, many in great detail, from business owners who needed advice on a range of topics; loans, benefits, licensing, etc.

I feel the year has been very productive for both of us. You've been a congenial and conscientious assistant and all of us have the highest regard for your abilities. Please feel free to call upon me for a recommendation if you require one for future employment.

Best of luck,
Thomas

1. What is NOT cited as part of Jean's work?
   (A) Organizing conferences
   (B) Processing business loans
   (C) Corresponding with clients
   (D) Maintaining a Web site

2. What does Thomas say about Jean?
   (A) She is a skillful writer
   (B) She is a diligent worker
   (C) She is an excellent teacher
   (D) She is an experienced supervisor

3. What does Thomas offer to do for Jean?
   (A) Raise her salary
   (B) Reduce her hours
   (C) Decrease her workload
   (D) Recommend her for a job

어휘 및 해석

Test 10 이메일

To: All families in our community
From: The San Jose Museum of Art

It's my pleasure to notify you that we are having our December Kids Art Sunday on December 11, 2007. With the objective of making the artwork on view accessible to young audiences, the Museum's Education Department will present a stimulating range of hands-on art workshops.

A speech by the curator Benito Juarez, gallery tours and other activities related to the current exhibitions will be also available to the visitors. There is no admission charge, and no reservations are required. However, you need to be at the Museum no later than 3p.m. if you do not want to miss a single event.

If you are interested in a setting with more one-on-one attention, join us for the member's only portions of Kids Art Sunday, *Side by Side.* It takes place in the SJ annex and includes a gallery discussion and structured hands-on art activities. Pre-registration is required for *Side by Side* and only one child is allowed per adult. To register or become a member, please call (408) 555-6867.

1. What are the visitors scheduled to do?
   (A) Attend a ceremony
   (B) View a performance
   (C) Listen to Mr. Juarez's talk
   (D) Visit gift shop for crafts

2. What is NOT necessary for visitors to attend Side by Side?
   (A) A membership
   (B) Admission fee
   (C) One child per adult guest
   (D) Reservations

어휘 및 해석

Test 11 이메일

To: Workshop leaders
From: Michelle Watkins, Micheile@FuturePlan.org
Subject: Innovations in Excellence Conference
Date: Tues., Nov 10

Everyone, here is the final schedule for the workshops during the conference. Please look it over and see if there are any problems. If you find an error, please notify me immediately.

Timetable

8:00A.M. Conference opens with a keynote speech by Jake Higgins in the Galaxy Auditorium

8:10A.M.-9:00A.M. Continental 13reakfast in the Island View Restaurant

9:00A.M. -9:30A.M. Organizational Meeting for workshop leaders- Room 202

9:30A.M.-11:00A.M.
Customer Service Workshop- Room 201
Networking and Contacts Workshop- Room 202
Dress for Success Workshop- Room 203
Effects of Sarnes-Baines Tax Law on Small Business Panel Discussion- Room 204

11:00A.M.-12.30P.M. Buffet Lunch in the Island View Restaurant and Free Time

12:30P.M.-2:00P.M.
Supply and Distribution Workshop- Room 201
Office Daycare Policies Workshop- Room 202
Effective Time Management Workshop- Room 203
Technology in the Workplace Panel discussion- Room 204

2:00P.M.-3:00P.M.
Speech by Sharon Westwood. CEO of Mercantile Bank- Grand Ballroom

1. Why was the e-mail written?
   (A) To provide a detailed schedule of an event
   (B) To request opinions for an event
   (C) To explain hotel reservations for an event
   (D) To five guidelines for participants

2. Where will the meeting for the recipients of this e-mail be held?
   (A) In the Galaxy Auditorium (B) In room 201
   (C) In room 202 (D) In room 203

3. Who is scheduled to deliver a closing speech to all participants?
   (A) Michelle Watkins (B) Jake Higgins
   (C) Sharon Westwood (D) The CEO of FuturePlan

어휘 및 해석

Test 12 편지

Frank Carridine
6200 N. Lake Shore Dr. Apt 1407
Chicago, IL 60656
Dear Mr. Carridine,

Thank you for contacting Amiga Electronics. We received your letter on May 17, 2007 asking for a Product Return Number (PRN) for the television that you purchased on April 26, 2007 at the Roger's Park Branch of Amiga Electronics.

Before we can issue you a PRN, there is some additional information that is required. Please mail us (phone calls and e-mail not accepted) a detailed explanation for why you wish to return the product as well as an indication that you have not used your Amiga HD television in a manner that voids your warranty. Once we have received the information, a customer service representative will be in contact with you.

Do not attempt to ship your item without a PRN as packages without PRNs are not accepted.

1. What item did Mr. Carridine want to return?
   (A) Video equipment
   (B) Exercise equipment
   (C) A telephone
   (D) A camera

2. How can Mr. Carridine obtain a PRN?
   (A) By calling a customer service representative
   (B) By providing some information by regular mail
   (C) By filling out a form on the company's website
   (D) By e-mailing the product's warranty number

어휘 및 해석

Test 13 이메일

From: Ellen Turner
To: Ned Alstock
Date: March 6, 2006
Subject: Retirement Party

Dear Ned,

As I'm sure you're well aware, we will be having a party to celebrate Samantha Wright' 30 years of service to the Haskell Corporation. All the details of the event have yet to be worked out, but I'll send you that information as soon as it is finalized.

I would like you to present Samantha with an award and make a short speech about her since you are the accounting department director and her immediate supervisor. It doesn't need to be very long.

A few words about how much she means to the department and how much she will be missed will suffice. If you have any questions, you can reach me at 555-9405.

Thank you.
Ellen

1. Who is Samantha Wright?
   (A) Ned Alstock's direct supervisor
   (B) An accounting department employee
   (C) A retired CEO of the Haskell Corporation
   (D) Ellen Turner's assistant

2. What is Mr. Alstock asked to do?
   (A) Help arrange a party
   (B) Conform his attendance
   (C) Make a presentation
   (D) Prepare a gift

어휘 및 해석

Test 14 편지

HK Electronics

September 28, 2009

Dear everyone;

The reason for my letter is to inform you that I have accepted the presidency of the Swift School of Business at Northern University and will be retiring as CEO of HK Electronics on October 31, 2009. I helped to found HK Electronics nearly 40 years ago, so the decision to leave has been tremendously difficult to make.

However, the company has grown to the point that I feel comfortable beginning the next chapter of my career, helping the next generation develop into the businesspeople of tomorrow.

During the past four decades here at HK, I have had the opportunity to work with a number of dedicated and skilled employees. I want to thank you all for the effort you have put into making HK the number one consumer electronics company in North America and I hope for your continued success.

Best Wishes,
Michael Carlson
CEO, HK Electronics

1. Who is the letter intended for?
   (A) Faculty at Northern University
   (B) Business acquaintances
   (C) Stockholders of HK Electronics
   (D) Coworkers at HK Electronics

2. What is the main purpose of this letter?
   (A) To recommend a new CEO
   (B) To announce the resignation of Mr. Carlson
   (C) To accept job offer
   (D) To discuss the company's progress

어휘 및 해석

Test 15 이메일

To: Mario Gonzalez mgonz@protemp.com
From: Estela Morales emorales@caixadirectcorp.com
Subject: Application
Date: July 20

Dear Mr. Gonzalez

Thank you for your application for the junior accounting position here at Caxia Direct. All application and resumes are first reviewed by two of our senior staff members. if you are selected for an interview following that review, you will be contacted by our personnel officer, Ricardo Martinez, who will set up an appointment. At that time, we will ask for names and contact information for three references.

Attached is a copy of our most recent annual report, as you requested. Thank you again for your interest, in .Caxia Direct Corporation.

Yours truly,
Estela

1. What is the purpose of the e-mail?
   (A) To inquire about an open position
   (B) To confirm receipt of an application
   (C) To request delivery of a document
   (D) To report on a first meeting

2. Who will contact Mr. Gonzalez to arrange a meeting?
   (A) The senior accountant
   (B) The record officer
   (C) The personnel officer
   (D) The office manager

3. What is being sent with the e-mail?
   (A) A bank statement
   (B) A staff directory
   (C) A company report
   (D) A job description

어휘 및 해석

Test 16 이메일

To: Office Depot service@officesupplies.com
From: Agatha Hill agatha0707@tsuma.com
Date: October 8
Subject: Order

To Whom It May Concern:

I ordered office desks and chairs from your online store two weeks ago. Unfortunately, the order I placed has not yet arrived where I wanted the delivery made. When I purchased these items, I was satisfied with your affordable prices and commitment to punctual delivery.

At that time, I expected them to shipped prior to the relocation of my office so I have to now require you to correct my address indicated in your customer directory. Please make a change in the previous address record. I attach a receipt of the purchase and a current address to this e-mail, I would appreciate it if you would send me a letter about the status of the order.

Sincerely
Agatha Hill

1. What is the purpose of the e-mail?
   (A) To inform a customer of the delay of an order
   (B) To notify Office Depot about some alterations
   (C) To inquire about the status of an order
   (D) To urge Agatha to change her address

2. What is sent with this e-mail?
   (A) A gift certificate
   (B) A receipt
   (C) An invoice
   (D) A letter

3. What is the recipient of this e-mail asked to do?
   (A) Cancel the Client's order
   (B) Call Agatha Hill immediately
   (C) Reflect the change of the shipment to a new address
   (D) Give a full refund

어휘 및 해석

Test 17 광고

Business World

For over twenty years, Business World has been the store for all of your need from pens and paper to computers and printers.

Business World's Copy Center is now open.

Black-and-white copies	$0.10 per page
Color copies	$0.15 per page
Business World preferred customers	10% off your total order

Store Hours:

Copies can be made while you wait or while you finish your shopping.

Sunday	11:00 A.M.-7:00 P.M.
Monday-Friday	8:00 A.M.-9:00 P.M
Saturday	9:30 A.M.-8:00 P.M

Business World
4276 Crove Blvd.
(Across from the 3rd St. train station)

1. What is the purpose of the advertisement?
   (A) To invite customers to a grand opening of a shop
   (B) To introduce a new service offered at a store
   (C) To announce the anniversary of a business
   (D) To promote a sale on selected items

2. When does the store close on Sunday?
   (A) At 7:00 P.M. (B) At 8:00 P.M
   (C) At 9:00 P:M · (D) At 9:30 P.M

어휘 및 해석

Test 18 광고

Valentino's Corner

895 Havana Circle
Toronto, Canada
Telephone: 905-555-7683

Serving the Greater Toronto area since 1970
Italian & North American dishes
Vegetarian food
Children's menu
Delicious ice cream desserts
Service provided by an experienced and courteous staff
Delivery & take-out service
***
Hours 8:00 A.M. -10:00 P.M. Sunday-Thursday
10:00AM-12:00 AM Friday & Saturday
Learn more about our menu on the Web at www.valenticnscorner.ca

1. What kind of business is Valentino's Corner?
(A) A restaurant
(B) A bakery
(C) A pottery shop
(D) A courier service

2. What information does NOT appear in the advertisement?
(A) T he types of offerings available to the establishment's customers
(B) T he hours during which the establishment is open
(C) How much items cost at the establishment
(D) How long the establishment has been in business

어휘 및 해석

Test 19 광고

Your fashion- your style

Welcome to Daisy Chain Fashion, Inc.

We specialize in brand name and boutique children's, women's and men's clothing and accessories.

What's new?
We have hundreds of 2007 fall/winter boutique clothing items coming in.

Holiday Clothing
We receive new holiday dresses and outfits every other day. Please check them out at our store.

Grand opening of our Online Store
Visit www. Daisychain.com now
Lots of specials for those who help us celebrate the opening of our new shop.

If you have any questions, please e-mail Stacy at Stacy@daisychain.com

1. What is the purpose of the advertisement?
(A) To recruit competent fashion designers
(B) To publicize new features of a store
(C) To inform people of the season's special events
(D) To announce a store's opening

2. What is NOT mentioned about Daisy Chain Fashion in the advertisement?
(A) Stacy is one of its employees dealing with customer inquiries
(B) It has recently started an online business
(C) It provides brand-name clothing at reduced prices
(D) T hey provide new products every other day

어휘 및 해석

Test 20 광고

Eurofleet understands that the only schedule that most businesspeople like to follow is their own. That is why, for our corporate club members, Eurofleet has introduced the first in-flight meal service that lets the customer decide when to eat.

If you are busy reviewing reports, writing important e-mails, taking a nap-or even if you are just not hungry - you are not required to eat on our schedule.

We will serve you a delicious meal at your convenience. Your meal will be prepared with the finest ingredients and served hot and fresh right to your seat.

1. What type of company is being advertised?
   (A) A restaurant
   (B) An airline
   (C) A business services center
   (D) A catering service

2. What special benefit is advertised?
   (A) A larger than usual selection of food
   (B) The use of a computer at no charge
   (C) Freedom to decide the time of a meal
   (D) Extra room in which to work

3. What is indicated about the benefit?
   (A) It can be requested by e-mail
   (B) It helps businesspeople save money
   (C) It is available to members of a club
   (D)It will become available soon

어휘 및 해석

Test 21 광고

Zumatech 3000 Hush Maker

Are you tired of daily chores? Do you think that keeping your floors and carpets in good condition should be easier and less exhausting? Do you find traditional vacuum cleaners too noisy?

Then the Zumatech 3000 is perfect for you. Our new Hush Maker noise-reduction technology makes the Zumatech 3000 ideal machine for home owners who appreciate top-quality products. Try one! You'll keep your floors spotless and your house peaceful!

1. What is being advertised?
   (A) A washing machine
   (B) A dishwasher
   (C) A clothes dryer
   (D) A vacuum cleaner

2. What is indicated about the product?
   (A) It is quiet.
   (B) It is inexpensive.
   (C) It is fast.
   (D) It saves energy.

어휘 및 해석

Test 22 광고

Peterman Piano Services
Family owned for 3 generations

* **Piano Tuning -** We tune grand, baby grand, upright, or spinet pianos
* **Restorations -** We bring older pianos back to their original beauty and sound quality.
* **Repairs -** We can fix almost any problem, including damage to parts or materials. If we do not have a part, we can order it.
* **Wood refinishing -** We can make your piano look new again.
* **Purchases -** We buy all types of pianos at excellent prices.
* **Additional Services -** We also provide piano-moving services throughout the area.

Our address is 23 East Broad Street in Bradford
And our telephone number is 670-555-0165

1. What is NOT a service offered by Peterman Piano Services?
   (A) Piano rental
   (B) Piano repair
   (C) Piano tuning
   (D) Piano moving

2. What is mentioned about Peterman Piano Services?
   (A) It sells new pianos.
   (B) It keeps piano parts in stock.
   (C) It offers discounts to schools.
   (D) It is a new company.

어휘 및 해석

Test 23 광고

Nelson's Blooms

Custom arrangements for any occasion

* Award-winning staff of 5 FSA-certified florists
* Area's largest selection of fresh flowers, stock arriving daily
* Nationwide delivery available, same day delivery within Piedmont Township during opening hours
* Large selection of plants
* Gift certificates and balloon bouquets available
* Open Monday-Saturday 10:00A.M.-9:00P.M.
* All major credit cards accepted
* Conveniently located in downtown Piedmont on Main Street
* Free parking available

Visit us or order by phone at 670-555-0122 or online at www.nelsonsblooms.com

1. What is mentioned about the staff at Nelson's blooms?
   (A) They have many years of experience.
   (B) They have won awards.
   (C) They grow the flowers they sell.
   (D) They are from Piedmont.

2. What does Nelson's Blooms NOT sell?
   (A) Balloons
   (B) Gift certificates
   (C) Plants
   (D) Gift baskets

3. What is indicated about delivery?
   (A) It is always completed on the day an order is placed.
   (B) It is available anywhere in the country.
   (C) It is offered every day of the week.
   (D) It is free for preferred customers.

어휘 및 해석

Test 24 광고

Flyte Bakery

All baked goods are handmade on the premise including

* Cakes
* Seasonal fruit pies
* Bread and pastries
* Cookies
* Personalized desserts for anniversaries, weddings, birthdays and other special occasions

Please order at least one week beforehand

Catering for corporate events and private parties is now available!
To learn more about our rates, telephone us during the business hours below

Monday-Saturday: 6 A.M . ~ 7 P.M.
Sunday: 6 A.M. ~ 6 P.M.

Location: 192 South Street, Sydney
Tel: (02) 9272-6555

1. What item would need to be ordered in advance?
(A) An autumn harvest apple pie (B) A personalized birthday cake
(C) Whole wheat bread (D) Chocolate chip cookies

2. For what information are customers directed to call the bakery?
(A) Store hours (B) Baking recipe
(C) Driving directions (D) Catering prices

어휘 및 해석

Test 25 광고

Lucy's Special Savings

We offer our regular customers a special discount on our various quality products including a variety of light bulbs, fluorescent lamps and electric lamps. Our products will illuminate your worktable and your private room.

Customers who have purchased our products more than three times over the last six months are eligible for this special offer. You can enjoy 30% off the regular prices for the products.

We are also planning to provide new customers with membership benefits without dues. If a new customer completes a membership form, a discount voucher for the next purchase will be presented.

Please note that during the sale, Lucy's will be open from 9 A.M. to 7 P.M. You can find locations near your residence on our Web site, www.Lucyillumanation.com.

1. What kind of business most likely is Lucy's store?
   (A) An office furniture supplier
   (B) A supplier of lighting fixtures
   (C) A supplier of kitchen appliances
   (D) A stationary store

2. What benefit will new customers get?
   (A) Special gifts
   (B) Registration for membership at a nominal cost
   (C) A complimentary voucher for next buying
   (D) A discount coupon for the next purchase

어휘 및 해석

Test 26 광고

Everyday Blossom Florist

We have been proudly serving the entire Sunset Valley since 1965. My grandparents opened this shop tight after they came back from their honeymoon. Ever since then, the shop has been a source of happiness to people in the neighborhood.

Just as my grandparents did, my parents go to the flower farm every other day to pick out the finest and the freshest flowers. My brothers and sisters trim and arrange the flowers perfectly for any type of event. Our family takes pride in serving its customers and doing so in the most pleasant way.

We are a family of professional florists, and we *offer t*he freshest and most elegant flower arrangements. We are always ready to satisfy your floral needs. We guarantee timely delivery. If your delivery arrives late, it's free. Please visit our online store at www.everydayblossom.com or visit our offline store anytime.

1. What is being advertised?
   (A) A family trip
   (B) A florist shop
   (C) A pizzeria
   (D) A gift shop

2. What is mentioned in the advertisement?
   (A) Refund on product damage
   (B) Sale on products
   (C) Timely delivery
   (D) Newly opened Web site

어휘 및 해석

Test 27 구인광고

Position: Financial Controller
Location of Position: Washington, DC

Our company is a successful and fast growing gas and electricity provider in this region. We are looking for a financial controller to replace two part-time roles and to free the Managing Director from his involvement in finance. The controller will have overall responsibility for the financial management of the company, including day-to-day financial accounting, as well as accurate and timely reporting on the profitability of individual projects and the company as a while.

Applicants should have a four-year degree in Accounting, and also a minimum of 5 years experience in accounts payable and receivable and general ledger accounting. Previous experience with the accounting program, STP, and advanced knowledge of Office programs would be an advantage. Experience in cash management and business planning is also required.

To apply for the position, please summit a cover letter and resume by February 15, 2010 to Recruitement@pep.com Successful applicants will be interviewed after March 1. Applicants will be notified with a decision by March 15, and will have to make a decision whether or not to accept the position with PEP by March 30.

1. Who is advertising the position?
   (A) A finance corporation
   (B) A utility company
   (C) An accounting firm
   (D) An IT company

2. What is NOT mentioned as a requirement for the position?
   (A) Computer proficiency in Office programs
   (B) A four-year accounting degree
   (C) At least 5 years of related experience
   (D) Previous experience in business planning

어휘 및 해석

Test 28 구인광고

Competent Graphic Designer Wanted

Modern & Practical Construction (MPC) is seeking a competent and enthusiastic graphic designer.
We, MPC, are one of the leading architectural companies in America. One of our employees won the Contemporary Architecture Prize in 2009.
The ideal applicant should have a bachelor's degree in a related field and at least five years of experience as a graphic designer. Proficiency in computer skills is a must. Fluent language skills are helpful but not required.

We offer qualified candidates opportunities to work in our foreign offices in London, Paris and Tokyo. Our benefits package includes a competitive salary, complimentary membership in a state-of-the-art fitness club and two weeks of annual leave of absence.

If you Intend to apply for the position, please send your resume, a cover letter and a letter of reference to Douglas Johnson, the director of the Human Resource Department.

1. What is the purpose of the advertisement?
   (A) To apply for a job
   (B) To accept an offer of employment
   (C) To advertise a newly released product
   (D) To seek a qualified worker

2. What is NOT one of the qualifications for the position?
   (A) Candidates should be college graduates
   (B) Candidates should be experienced in a related field.
   (C) Fluent language skills are required.
   (D) Applicants should have proficient computer skills.

3. What is the benefit provided by. MPC?
   (A) Free gym membership
   (B) Complimentary housing
   (C) An opportunity to get a promotion
   (D) The position of the head of the graphic design team

어휘 및 해석

Test 29 구인광고

Job Opportunity
The Head of Accounting Department
Starting from January 1

Requirements for the position are as follows: at least four years of experience in a related field, a certificate in accounting and fluency in both English and Korean.
Only qualified candidates will be taken into consideration for an interview with executives of our company.

As the head accountant, you will be supervise the accounting staff members ensuring that they comply with auditing regulations, reviewing the accuracy of accounting materials and checking the appropriateness of our budget proposals.

Remuneration will be commensurate with experience and achievements.
However, there is room to negotiate compensation and concrete benefits.
Applicants should submit an indicating a desirable salary range, a salary history and a resume. In addition, please note that proof of all credentials must be included.

1. What is the purpose of the information?
   (A) To reject an offer of employment
   (B) To provide special offers
   (C) To announce a job vacancy
   (D) To inquire about an .offer of employment

2. What is the one of the requirements to be hired for the job?
   (A) Bilingual communication skills
   (B) A bachelor's degree
   (C) Three years of experience in accounting
   (D) Knowledge of auditing regulation

어휘 및 해석

Test 30 구인광고

Part-time Wedding Hall Guide Needed!

The Grand hotel has finally finished renovating its wedding hall and is more than ready to fulfill the dreams of all brides and grooms. In order to do so, we are looking for men and women who have a cheery personality to assist the wedding ceremonies.

You will have to work only during weekends. For sudden Friday night weddings, you might be pages for quick support. But in these cases, you will be paid 20% more than your usual weekend fees.

No job experience is necessary. So all you need is a bright smile and a polite attitude! But you do need to submit your resume and describe why you are willing to work for our hotel as a wedding hall guide. Please submit your resume to Michael Park by the end of this month.

Mary Southern
Grand Hotel

1. What position is being offered in the advertisement?
(A) Receptionist (B) Wedding planner
(C) Sales associate (D) Wedding assistant

2. According to the advertisement, what qualification is NOT preferred?
(A) Politeness (B) Previous experience
(C) Willingness to work on Fridays (D) Cheerfulness

어휘 및 해석

Test 31 구인광고

Sunnyvale Restaurant Corporation, an award-winning fine dining restaurant chain for fifty years, has an immediate opening for a marketing intern based in our San Francisco office. The individual will update and maintain a customer database and upload the database to our e-mail system monthly.

Sunnyvale Restaurant Corporation is a restaurant and bar chain with 7000 employees and 280 locations, and plans worldwide expansion and hiring in a push to open more than 30 locations this year.

REQUIREMENTS

Competence in writing marketing copy
0utstanding communications skills (both written and verbal)
Bilingual in English-French

Please write for an application form to:
Personnel Department
Sunnyvale Restaurant Corporation

1. Where will the successful candidate work?
   (A) In a bar
   (B) In a food company
   (C) In a restaurant
   (D) In an office

2. What is mentioned as a requirement for the job?
   (A) Prior experience in a related field
   (B) Fluency in two languages
   (C) A graduate degree
   (D) Good computer skills

어휘 및 해석

Test 32 구인광고

MARKETING ASSOCIATE WANTED
COMPUTER SOFTWARE

An internationally-recognized software company is currently seeking a marketing associate for the Seattle area.

The ideal candidate will have a degree in business administration and have a minimum of two years professional experience relating to marketing computer software at the corporate level. Familiarity with computer programming and language ability in Japanese and/or French are important skills.

The company is willing to propose a strong initial offer to such a candidate, Including stock options, furnished accommodation, use of a company vehicle, a comprehensive health coverage plan, and an expense account. Preliminary interviews will occur on May 15-18 for qualified applicants. Please send your resume to:

Milton Software Ltd.
P.O. Box 234
Seattle, Washington

1. What does the company require?
   (A) Ability to communicate in Spanish
   (B) Being trilingual
   (C) Corporate marketing experience
   (D) Two pieces of photo-identification

2. What benefit does the company offer?
   (A) Health *coverage*
   (B) Unemployment insurance
   (C) Coverage for family education expenses
   (D) A new computer

어휘 및 해석

Test 33 구인광고

Wanted: Recent College Grads!

Modern Mode & Co. is looking for recent college graduates to fill a number of sales associate positions at the largest clothing retail stores throughout the Los Angeles area.

No experience is necessary but applicants must be recent college graduates and have a positive attitude. Knowledge of high fashion is not required, but candidates must like fashion and have an eagerness to learn.

Applicants must interact with clients in a polite and professional manner while making customers' purchases and being aware of all promotions and sale items.

We offer a *very* competitive salary and health benefits package, in-house discounts on all store articles, an eight-hour work day and two weeks of paid vacation.

If interested please send your resume and *cover* letter to:
jessicajordan@modernmode.com. Write "Sales Associate" in the subject line.

1. What position is being offered?
   (A) Fashion Designer
   (B) Store manager
   (C) cashier
   (D) Sales Representative

2. What is NOT listed as a benefit of joining the company?
   (A) Health insurance
   (B) Paid vacations
   (C) Flexible working hours
   (D) Discounts

어휘 및 해석

Test 34 구인광고

Recruitment

Good Life Insurance Inc. is seeking an experienced sales representative. As we are planning to open a new office in Los Angeles, we will employ a group of regular staff members. The procedure for recruitment includes a serried of steps: screening of qualifications including a resume, a cover letter and a letter of reference, An English interview and an interview with executives.

All candidates should have previous experience related to sales and marketing. In addition, they are required to be equipped with good communication skills to deal with customers' claims.

Within one week, we will confirm receipt of required documents. The, successful candidates will get a call from the HR department to arrange an Interview.

Please send application materials by e-mail to the director of the HR department:
winifredsharp@recruitment.com.

1. Which position is available now?
   (A) Sales director
   (B) Salesperson
   (C) Graphic designer
   (D) Accountant

2. What is NOT one of the qualifications for the position?
   (A) Good interpersonal skills
   (B) Prior experience
   (C) The record of winning a prize
   (D) An acquaintance's recommendation

어휘 및 해석

Test 35 공지

Comtex Credit Card Buyer Protection Plan

As a Comtex cardholder, you are automatically covered by the Buyer Protection Plan, which insures purchases made with your credit card for a fell 90 days from the date of purchase.

The Buyer Protection Plan provides insurance for loss or theft of, and accidental damage to, covered items purchased with your card anywhere in the worJd. The amount of coverage is limited to the amount charged to your Comtex credit card for the items.

To file a claim, call 55509143. Failure to give notice within 45 days of the date of loss or damage may result in denial of your claim. Once you report a loss, a Comtex credit associate will set up a claim file for you and send you a claim form. You must send the completed form along with all requested documentation to the claims within 60 days of your receipt of the claim form.

1. When does insurance coverage take effect?
   (A) When the cardholder applies for it
   (B) As soon as the buyer calls the credit associate
   (C) 90 days after a credit card in issued
   (D) On the day an item is purchased with the card

2. How much insurance for a single item is provided by the plan?
   (A) Half the item's current cost
   (B) The original item cost charged to the card
   (C) The cost of the item less a service fee
   (D) The current replacement cost of the item

3. How soon after an item is lost must a cardholder notify the company?
   (A) Within 7 days
   (B) Within 45 days
   (C) Within 60 days
   (D) Within 90 days

어휘 및 해석

Test 36 공지

Special Summer Offer!

Members of the Pendleton gym can take advantage of a new special *offer* this summer.

Monthly passes to the West Springfield Swim Center are available at a 50 percent discount Pendleton members.

Passes can be purchased at the gym office in Room2, which is open from 9 A.M. to 3 P.M.

To receive the discount, members must show a valid membership card.

1. What is being announced?
   (A) Longer pool hours
   (B) Additional membership fees
   (C) Reduced admission rates
   (D) Free swimming lessons

2. What are people asked to bring to the gym office?
   (A) A receipt
   (B) An application form
   (C) A coupon
   (D) A membership card

어휘 및 해석

Test 37 공지

Computer donations requested!

The Filemore Community Center is asking for donations of used computers. T he center will gladly accept any desktop or laptop computers, provided that they are still functional. Computer accessories will also be welcome. However, we do not have any need for printers at this time. Please drop off any donations at the front desk of the community center. These computers will be used for adult community classes on basic computer center's classes are free for the Filemore community. Classes are scheduled to begin in January.

Please call 555-0319 for more details.

1. What would most likely NOT be accepted as a donation?
   (A) An old laptop computer
   (B) A used computer keyboard
   (C) A working printer
   (D) A working monitor

2. How will the donation be used?
   (A) To teach children how to use computers
   (B) To train adults in computer skills
   (C) To provide computers to needy families
   (D) To supply local schools with computers

어휘 및 해석

Test 38 공지

Northwood Community Center

March Employee of the Month

Employee: Linda Ahn
Classes: Watercolor Painting
Pen and Ink Drawing
Interest: Photography

Art instructor Linda Ahn is one of the most popular figures at our community center. She teaches on Tuesday and Saturday mornings and Thursday nights, and her classes are usually filled to capacity.
In May she is going to start teaching an afternoon beginner's drawing class on Mondays and Wednesdays.

Linda began teaching here last July, but her creative talents have taken her in many directions. Before teaching here she was a costume designer for the Copenhagen Theater Company for three years. Linda is also an accomplished amateur photographer who has taken pictures of the many places she has visited while touring with the theater group. She displayed some of them in the Town Hall gallery in October.

So sign up for one of Linda's classes - you'll be glad you did!

1. On what day of the week does Linda Ahn teach an evening class?
(A) On Monday (B) On Tuesday
(C) On Wednesday (D) On Thursday

2. According to the information, what will happen in May?
(A) A new employee will start working. (B) An afternoon class will begin meeting.
(C) The building will close for renovations. (D) Enrollment for classes will resume

어휘 및 해석

Test 39 공지

SPACE AVAILABLE

8505 Freeport Parkway provides 12000 square meters of luxury space set on a large, beautifully landscaped lot. The finished site consists of two 12-story office towers, a four-level parking garage, and a restaurant.
This site located in a highly visible location near the rapidly growing residential area of Meltonville. For information on leasing, please call Michiko Watanabe at 555-0183.

1. For whom is the notice primarily intended?
   (A) People who want to buy a house in Meltonville
   (B) Landscape designer
   (C) Real estate developers
   (D) Businesspeople looking for office space

2. Who most likely is Michiko Watanabe?
   (A) A restaurant owner
   (B) An interior decorator
   (C) A rental agent
   (D) A city planner

어휘 및 해석

Test 40 공지

From the office of
Doctor Calvin Hoffman
27 Shilling Road Canton, IL 61520
(309) 555-0128

Because your health is important to us, we would like to remind you that it's time for your examination. We look forward to seeing you!

□ your appointments is on *Monda□ September 8 at 8:30 A.M.*

Note: If you cannot keep your appointment, please provide at least 24 hours advance notice or you will be charged a fee.

1. Why was the notice sent?
   (A) To advertise a doctor's services
   (B) To cancel a meeting
   (C) To remind a patient about an appointment
   (D) To inform a doctor of a telephone call

2. What is mentioned about the doctor's office?
   (A) It has openings for new patients.
   (B) It charges a fee for late cancellations.
   (C) It is no longer open on Mondays
   (D) It calls people 24 hours before their visit.

어휘 및 해석

Test 41 공지

Filter Maintenance

The Desna drinking water filter guarantees clean drinking water from your faucet, provided that a new cartridge is inserted into the filter once every six months. The procedure is easy and safe to perform if the following points are observed.

*Before you replace your old cartridge, make sure that the water is off. Turn the main faucet tightly until it has stopped dripping.
*Remember that your spare cartridge is enclosed in the package that came with the filter. New cartridges may be purchased anywhere Desna products are sold.

Before you open the old filter for replacement, you may need to allow the water inside it to cool. Do not drain the filter or remove the cartridge before you are sure it has cooled down.

1. What are the instructions for?
   (A) Cleaning old faucets
   (B) Heating the water in the filter
   (C) Replacing filter cartridge
   (D) Measuring water temperature

2. What should user do first?
   (A) Clean the cartridge
   (B) Remove the filter
   (C) Turn off the water
   (D) Replace the faucet

3. According to the instructions, why should users be careful during the process?
   (A) The water may be hot.
   (B) The device is very fragile.
   (C) The tools used are sharp.
   (D) Dirty water may spill from faucet.

어휘 및 해석

Test 42 공지

Waste prevention sales resources and money. Begin by examining the waste you generate and where it comes from. T hen look for ways to improve efficiency and eliminate waste. T he ideas below can help you get started.

Writing/ Printing Paper

Make double-sided copies whenever possible.
Reuse envelops and use two-way envelopes.
Circulate memos, periodicals, and reports rather than distributing individual copies.
Use voice or electronic mail or post memos on a central bulletin board.
Save documents on disks instead of printing hard copies.
Proof documents on screen before printing.

Equipment

Rent equipment that is used only occasionally instead of buying.
Use remanufactured office equipment.
Invest in equipment that facilitates waste prevention, such as: high quality, durable, repairable equipment.
Institute regular maintenance practices that prolong the life of copiers, computers and other equipment.
Reclaim reusable parts from old equipment.
Use refilled or rebuilt fax and printer cartridges.

Donate and Exchange

Donate old magazines or journals to hospitals or clinics
Donate unwanted supplies to local schools, libraries, or nonprofit organizations.
Advertise surplus and reusable items through a commercial materials exchange.

1. What is the notice mainly about?
   (A) Energy saving
   (B) Environmental conservation
   (C) Separate garbage collection
   (D) Waste reduction

2. What is NOT a suggested way to decrease the amount of paper thrown away?
   (A) Put up saving guidelines on bulletin boards.
   (B) Make copies on both sides of papers.
   (C) Pass circulars
   (D) Use electronic mail.

3. What is recommended as a way to increase the durability of equipment?
(A) Purchasing proper sized equipment
(B) Recycling reusable equipment parts
(C) Having equipment inspected regularly
(D) Choosing power saving parts for equipment

4. According to the notice, where can publications be donated?
(A) To libraries
(B) To hospitals
(C) To schools
(D) To branches

어휘 및 해석

Test 43 공지

let Builder's Advantage Work for you!

Obtain your share in the marketplace by advertising in

Builders Advantage Magazine

* Glossy, large-format magazine dedicated to the construction industry
* Four issues annually
* Readership of over 40,000
* Distributed to over 250 area businesses in Farmington and Uxbridge countries
* Quarter-and half-page advertisements available
* Advertisements start as low as $150.00
* Discounts offered on advertisements placed in multiple issues

Call our public relations Department at 055-1043 for details.

1. What is being offered in the notice?
   (A) Construction services
   (B) A building for rent
   (C) Advertising space
   (D) Magazine subscriptions

2. What is indicated about *Builders Advantage Magazine?*
   (A) It is distributed to homes.
   (B) It is published four times a year.
   (C) It contains full-page advertisements.
   (D) It is a new magazine.

어휘 및 해석

Test 44 메모

OFFICE MESSAGE

TO: Takashi Matsumoto
FROM: Karen Lang
TIME: 9:30, Thursday, July 22, 2010

Telephone Fax Office Visit

MESSAGE:

Karen Lang from C&P Accounting called. She wants to arrange a new meeting time with you.
Instead of on Monday at 11. can you see her on Tuesday at 1:30?
She'll be able to go over the contract with you then.
She'll try to contact you again this afternoon.

Taken By: Mike Nguyen

1. Why did Ms. Lang call Mr. Matsumoto?
   (A) To reschedule an appointment with him
   (B) To ask if he will be able to meet a deadline
   (C) To inquire where a meeting will take place
   (D) To request that he send a new contract

2. What will Ms. Lang probably do?
   (A) See Mr. Matsumoto on Monday
   (B) Call Mr. Matsumoto again this afternoon
   (C) Contact a representative of C&P Accounting
   (D) Make a reservation for a lunch meeting

어휘 및 해석

Test 45 메모

Date: January 28
To: Building M Community
From: Janis T ing, Director of the Office Space committee
Subject: Jay Yoon auditorium Renovation

We wanted to alert you to the fact that the renovation of the Jay yoon Auditorium, the first Phase of a two-phase project, will begin in mid-February. The second phase, reconstruction of the first-floor offices adjacent to the auditorium, could begin as early as August, with an intended completion date of late November.

A project of this scope, in such a central location, will necessarily cause a certain degree of disruption to our community, and every effort will be made to minimize this disruption. Plans have already been made to provide alternative venues during alternative venues, inform Lidia Ibrahim (Ext. 3372, librahim@m.galleries.com) as soon as possible.

Should there time lines change in any way at this work progresses; we will keep the community informed. We greatly appreciate your patience as we continue to enhance our facilities.

1. Why was the memo written?
   (A) To announce alternative venues
   (B) To warn about possible disruptions
   (C) To revise the schedule for a project
   (D) To inform employees about new staff

2. What does the second phase of the renovation involve?
   (A)Adding another floor
   (B) Reconstructing office space
   (C) Centralizing event facilities
   (D) Upgrading an adjacent building

3. When is the project expected to be completed?
   (A) In January
   (B) In February
   (C) In August
   (D) In November

어휘 및 해석

Test 46 메모

Memo

To: All employees
From: Marsha Gray, Business Manager
Date: Oct 5
Subject: Copy Machines

A copying machine has been placed next to the staff lounge. You may use it to copy your brochures, ticket. information, customer itineraries, and reservation confirmations. You can find extra paper in the supply room. Do not allow customers to use the machine.

If you have to make more than 25 photocopies, please use the high-speed copier located on the second floor. In any case, you should make your own copies and not ask the administrative assistants to do it.

Should a copy machine require repair or_ maintenance, please contact Trish Leslie in the accounting office (555-1664, extension 470) and she will notify the manufacturer.

1. What kind of company does Marsha Gray most likely work for?
   (A) A computer company
   (B) A copy machine manufacturer
   (C) An accounting firm
   (D) A travel agency

2. What should employees notify if one of the copiers needs service?
   (A) The copier manufacturer
   (B) An administrative assistant
   (C) Trish Leslie
   (D) Marsha Gray

어휘 및 해석

부록

GRAMMAR ANSWER

20 – 21 p 품사 실전문제

1.D 2.A 3.C 4.C 5.C 6.B 7.B 8.B 9.A 10.C

27 – 28 p 동사 실전문제

1.D 2.A 3.D 4.A 5.B 6.B 7.C 8.C 9.B 10.A

31 – 33 p 수의 일치 실전문제

1.B 2.A 3.A 4.B 5.B 6.B 7.D 8.D 9.D 10.A 11.D 12.B 13.B 14.C 15.B 16.B 17.A 18.B 19.A 20.A

39 – 41 p 시제 실전문제

1.D 2.C 3.B 4.C 5.C 6.C 7.A 8.C 9.B 10.C 11.C 12.C 13.C 14.D 15.D 16.A 17.A 18.C 19.A 20.B

46 – 48 p 수동태 실전문제

1.A 2.A 3.C 4.A 5.A 6.A 7.B 8.A 9.B 10.C 11.A 12.B 13.A 14.D 15.C 16.C 17.D 18.B 19.B 20.B

51 – 53 p 가정법 실전문제

1.C 2.A 3.D 4.B 5.C 6.D 7.C 8.A 9.A 10.B 11.C 12.A 13.B 14.B 15.B 16.C 17.B 18.B 19.B 20.B

58 – 60 p to부정사 실전문제

1.C 2.B 3.C 4.A 5.C 6.C 7.C 8.A 9.D 10.A 11.A 12.D 13.D 14.D 15.B 16.C 17.B 18.C 19.A 20.D

63 – 65 p 동명사 실전문제

1.B 2.D 3.B 4.A 5.B 6.A 7.C 8.C 9.C 10.D 11.C 12.B 13.A 14.B 15.D 16.A 17.D 18.B 19.B 20.B

71 - 73 p 분사 실전문제

1.A 2.B 3.A 4.A 5.C 6.B 7.A 8.B 9.D 10.B 11.B 12.C 13.B 14.A 15.B 16.B 17.D 18.D 19.C 20.A

80 - 82 p 등위, 부사절 접속사 실전문제

1.C 2.D 3.A 4.D 5.A 6.B 7.D 8.B 9.A 10.B 11.B 12.A 13.A 14.C 15.A 16.B 17.A 18.C 19.B 20.D

86 - 88 p 명사절 접속사 실전문제

1.A 2.B 3.B 4.A 5.A 6.B 7.A 8.C 9.A 10.C 11.A 12.B 13.A 14.A 15.C 16.C 17.A 18.A 19.D 20.B

92 - 94 p 형용사절 접속사 실전문제

1.C 2.A 3.B 4.C 5.B 6.A 7.A 8.B 9.A 10.A 11.C 12.A 13.B 14.C 15.A 16.A 17.A 18.A 19.A 20.D

95p. E-mail
1.B 2.D

96p. Letter
1.C 2.A

97-98p. E-mail
1.B 2.D

99p. Letter
1.B 2.C 3.B

100p. Information
1.D 2.A

101p.Notice
1.D 2.D

102p. Advertisement
1.C 2.D

독해 실전문제

Test 1
1.D 2.C

Test 2
1.D 2.C

Test 3
1.D 2.B

Test 4
1.B 2.A

Test 5
1.D 2.D 3.A

Test 6
1.D 2.B

Test 7
1.C 2.B

Test 8
1.D 2.C

Test 9
1.B 2.B 3.D

Test 10
1.C 2.B

Test 11
1.A 2.C 3.C

Test 12
1.A 2.B

Test 13
1.B 2.C

Test 14
1.D 2.B

Test 15
1.B 2.C 3.C

Test 16
1.C 2.B 3.C

Test 17
1.B 2.A

Test 18
1.A 2.C

Test 19
1.B 2.C

Test 20
1.B 2.C 3.C

Test 21
1.D 2.A

Test 22
1.A 2.B
Test 23
B 2.D 3.B

Test 24
1.B 2.D

Test 25
1.B 2.D

Test 26
1.B 2.C

Test 27
1.B 2.A

Test 28
1.D 2.C 3.A

Test 29
1.C 2.A

Test 30
1.D 2.B

Test 31
1.D 2.B

Test 32
1.C 2.A

Test 33
1.D 2.C

Test 34
1.B 2.C

Test 35
1.D 2.B 3.B

Test 36
1.C 2.D

Test 37
1.C 2.B
Test 38
1.D 2.B 3.A

Test 39
1.D 2.C

Test 40
1.C 2.B

Test 41
1.C 2.C 3.A

Test 42
1.D 2.A 3.C 4.B

Test 43
1.C 2.B

Test 44
1.A 2.A

Test 45
1.B 2.B 3.D

Test 46
1.D 2.C

기본기를 다지기 위한

Practical English

2022년 02월 05일 초판 1쇄발행
2023년 02월 25일 초판 2쇄 발행
2023년 09월 04일 초판 3쇄 발행

저 자:김태훈
발행인 : 유 수 경
발행처 : 도서출판 영민

등 록 : 2001. 7. 16 제1-2888호
주 소 : 서울시 성북구 보문로 58-1 한주빌딩 205호
전 화 : 02-904-7204
팩 스 : 02-921-7202

ISBN 978-89-6341-338-9 13740

값 14,000원